W9-ARF-255

Jacobson, Beverly.

Young programs for
older workers

DATE			
NOV 0 1 2008			

YOUNG PROGRAMS FOR OLDER WORKERS

YOUNG PROGRAMS FOR OLDER WORKERS

Case Studies in Progressive Personnel Policies

Beverly Jacobson

Van Nostrand Reinhold/Work in America Institute Series

VAN NOSTRAND REINHOLD COMPANY
NEW YORK   CINCINNATI   ATLANTA   DALLAS   SAN FRANCISCO
LONDON   TORONTO   MELBOURNE

Van Nostrand Reinhold Company Regional Offices:
New York   Cincinnati   Atlanta   Dallas   San Francisco

Van Nostrand Reinhold Company International Offices:
London   Toronto   Melbourne

Manufactured in the United States of America

Published by Van Nostrand Reinhold Company
135 West 50th Street, New York, N.Y. 10020

Published simultaneously in Canada by Van Nostrand Reinhold Ltd.
15   14   13   12   11   10   9   8   7   6   5   4   3   2   1

Library of Congress Cataloging in Publication Data

Jacobson, Beverly.
   Young programs for older workers.

   (Van Nostrand Reinhold/Work in America Institute
series)
   Includes index.
   1. Aged—Employment—United States—Case
studies. 2. Personnel management—United States—
Case studies. I. Title. II. Series.

HD6280.J3   658.3'042   80-12621
ISBN 0-442-25405-9

VNR/WORK IN AMERICA INSTITUTE SERIES

The VNR/Work in America Institute Series is designed to provide practical insight into new and better ways to advance productivity and the quality of working life. The objective is to create heightened awareness of the opportunities for an enriched work life that can exist in innovative organizations, and to reveal the benefits of linking people and production in a common goal, through clearer understanding of the key factors contributing to worker output and job satisfaction.

The Series will provide guidance on a number of concerns that influence work performance, not only in today's work environment, but also in the even more complex world of work that lies ahead. Titles in the World of Work Series will focus on five fundamental issues affecting the work community: (1) *The quality of working life,* exploring opportunity, recognition, participation, and rewards for employees to optimize their involvement in and contribution to the work organization; (2) *Productivity,* focusing on the human factors in the productivity equation, to increase both individual and organizational output through more effective use of human resources; (3) *Education and the world of work,* discussing ways to improve the match between the entry-level worker and the job, by building bridges from education to the world of work; (4) *Employee-management cooperation,* recognizing that employees contribute important know-how and ingenuity to increase output, reduce waste, maintain product quality, and improve morale; and (5) *National labor force policy,* examining policies of the United States and other industrialized nations as they affect productivity and the quality of working life.

Foreword

Recent changes in the law that forbid discrimination on the basis of age, and move the age of mandatory retirement from 65 to 70 in the private sector have alerted many firms, including those which have never had mandatory retirement, to the need for new policies regarding older workers.

It is our belief that employers, by and large, want to take a progressive stance toward older employees. But with the realization that it is as illegal to show favor as to discriminate against these workers, employers are looking for policies that benefit employees of all ages, *including* older ones.

This casebook aims to meet a need which became clear when, as part of a national policy study on older workers, "The Future of Older Workers in America," we conducted a survey of the Fortune 1300 companies and a number of other companies with which Work in America Institute has had contact. The number of respondents who indicated they were actually conducting programs that took older workers' special needs into consideration proved to be smaller than the number who said, in effect, "We're not doing anything of particular interest in this area, but we're eager to hear what others are doing."

In response to the apparent need, we present here close to 70 examples of progressive policies currently in effect among a wide variety of employers. The reports are written for the intelligent layperson. They contain a minimum of jargon and a great deal of concrete detail. In some cases the programs described here are geared directly to the needs of older workers; in others, the programs are more general in nature, but have special applicability to older workers.

The book stands on its own merits, but it is also designed to be read in conjunction with *The Future of Older Workers in America*, the policy study report published by Work in America Institute in 1980. The two volumes illuminate each other: one reports particular programs in operation today, the other attempts to forecast major social, economic, and demographic changes for the 1980s and to recommend new perspectives and policies to improve the productivity and quality of work life of older workers.

We are grateful to the Rockefeller Brothers Fund and to the Commonwealth Fund for underwriting the 18-month policy study which produced the casebook and the report.

JEROME M. ROSOW
President
Work in America Institute, Inc.

An Overview

The research for this volume describing *Young Programs for Older Workers* started with a blank piece of paper, that is, without preconceived notions. Unlike the Work in America Institute policy study *The Future of Older Workers in America,* which this book complements, the emphasis here has been not on theory but on actual practice—not on what should be, but on what is. The motivation for compiling this information had nothing whatever to do with social reform. It arose, rather, from an interest in identifying progressive personnel interventions by business organizations whose bottom line is profitability, and government programs designed to move workers toward economic independence. Some of these programs were designed specifically for older workers; others were planned to cover the general population but are well suited to the needs of older workers.

A questionnaire was sent to 1300 companies requesting information on personnel policies affecting older employees in the following areas: hiring and firing, employing annuitants, flexible work schedules, permanent part-time work, job sharing, redesign of jobs, demotion, retraining, continuing education, educational leaves and sabbaticals, second careers, performance evaluation, salary and pay practices, and benefits.

Ninety-one companies responded, a return of 7 percent. Work in America Institute consultants and staff, as well as members of the policy study's national advisory committee, provided additional leads. Marc Rosenblum and Harold L. Sheppard graciously supplied their list of 43 companies *(Jobs for Older Workers in U.S. Industry: Possibilities and Prospects.* [Washington, D.C.: American Institutes for Research, 1977]). In all, more than 170 organizations provided the data base for this project. The final 69 units represent a cross-section of what industry and government are doing in the area of the older worker. The universe is substantial; these organizations contain a *total* population in excess of 2.5 million workers.

Considerable interest exists in this subject. Representatives of two dozen companies with no data to contribute took time to write, and they asked for the study results. These requests came from heavy industry (autos, steel, mining), high-technology corporations, banks, insurance and oil companies, and hotel chains.

In-depth, multiple telephone interviews were used to collect information, and often more than one representative of a company or program was interviewed. The individuals interviewed were policy makers— personnel directors, vice-presidents of industrial relations or human resources departments, directors of retiree relations or compensation and benefits, and heads of government programs.

Dominant concepts emerged as the cases were considered by Work in America Institute staff. As a result, the book was organized into six sections dealing with new work arrangements, reentry workers, secondary organizations, redeployment, hiring older workers and annuitants, and assessing and advising them.

1 New Work Arrangements

Part-time work, phased retirement, and second-career training represent three new working arrangements that are responses to changes in the economy. While retailers have used part-time employees for years to cover their longer-than-average working weeks, other industries are rethinking their policies in this area. A utility in the Midwest wants to regularize part-time employment and provide such workers with career paths and benefits as a way of streamlining its operation, improving productivity, and attracting new groups of workers. A rapidly growing manufacturer of home maintenance equipment is considering upgrading its part-time benefits package to attract higher caliber employees. Conversely, to deal with the shrinking profession of teaching, the states of California and Kansas have made a substantial breakthrough in work-sharing by changing pension rules to allow older teachers to collect their full pensions while working part time.

Other private-sector companies are flirting with phased retirement. Here the problem is to find a way for employees to reduce their working life gradually without decreasing pension benefits. The problem requires a solution, and it must be found quickly in order to deal with what many regard as the wave of the future.

Second-career training is another option that can extend working life through a series of contiguous careers. It is important that these programs be well planned and implemented, conducted by experts, and tied to marketplace needs. The poor success rate of the second-careers program for air traffic controllers reflects the lack of sufficient counseling, improper screening of participants, and inadequate attention to the age factor.

2   Reentry Workers

Typical reentry workers are women who left the labor force to raise families and then returned to work after varying periods of time. The cases in this section deal with government programs designed to help women toward economic independence.

Since only 4.6 percent of the nation's small businesses are owned by women, the American Woman's Economic Development Corporation was established to train women entrepreneurs in business skills. A 1979 survey of program participants showed a collective increase in their net sales of more than $17 million.

The career facilitation projects of the National Science Foundation were established to upgrade the skills of women with degrees in math and science. Since 1976, 1000 women have attended 21 programs. Sixty-five percent have found jobs as scientists and engineers in the private sector, and another 10 percent are in graduate school. These successful pilot programs are now looking for new sources of funding. Support from industry, foundations, professional societies, and the academic community is being investigated.

The displaced homemaker programs are a response to the social and economic dislocation caused by the high divorce rate. Since estimates put the number of displaced homemakers at the 4 million mark, these efforts represent only a first step in dealing with this problem.

3   Secondary Organizations

The fact that many annuitants desire employment is no longer open to question. Forty-six percent of retirees surveyed by a 1979 Harris poll said they would prefer to be working, and secondary organizations that help older workers find jobs all report increased demand. Employers who hire older workers and annuitants are increasingly pleased with their reliability and performance. The problem seems to lie in matching their skills with existing needs. Several organizations are trying to establish data banks to facilitate this matching process.

One secondary organization has had particular success placing older CETA workers. A surprising 95.6 percent of participants over the age of 50 who have attended the three-week Job Finders workshop have obtained employment in the private sector, and 81 percent of them have retained these positions for at least six months. This self-directed placement program teaches participants what the business world expects of them, while leaving the responsibility for the job search completely in their hands.

4   Redeployment

This section deals with the involuntary movement of workers because of changing economic and technological conditions. Increasingly, corporate employers who are forced to terminate executives and salaried personnel are providing outplacement counseling to speed up the job relocation process and ease the trauma of separation. In spite of the severe problems which accompany the loss of a job, statistics from two studies by professional outplacement counselors show that over 70 percent of terminated employees get better paying jobs when they relocate. However, older workers have a significantly harder time both in accepting the job loss and in finding new positions.

Age seems to affect a manager's attitude toward demotion. A 1978 survey of Danish managers showed that the older the employees, the more likely they are to accept transfers to positions of lesser responsibility and pay. While there has been little acceptance of, and experience with, demotion in this country, in corporations where it has worked, as at Kellogg and Maremont, several important principles have been observed. The reassignment was mutually agreed upon by employer and employee, the employee was included in the planning process from the beginning, time was allowed to explore other options, the final choice was left to the employee, and, where possible, the reassignment involved transfer to another unit within the company.

5   The New "New Hires"—Older Workers

Older workers and annuitants are being hired by high-technology industries, banks and insurance companies, and manufacturers. Where skills are in short supply, in the fields of engineering and computer technology, secretarial and clerical work, and skilled craft areas, age is not a limiting factor. Employers are finding that older workers are reliable and productive, and some companies, notably Bankers Life and Casualty Company, are saving employment agency fees by establishing on-call work forces of their own for their annuitants. While some older workers and annuitants return to work full time, the vast majority work as consultants and part-time employees, supplementing their retirement income. According to Donald Walker, employee relations manager at Pennsylvania Power and Light Company, the changes which have allowed older workers back into the labor force are partly legal (the effect of the amendment to the Age Discrimination in Employment Act), partly technical (the need for their skills), and partly attitudinal (a new managerial sensitivity to the whole question of aging).

6   Assessing and Advising

Four kinds of assessment and advice are covered in this final section. The most complex deals with performance appraisal. Although there is little agreement about the accuracy of various appraisal techniques, there are some dominant themes. Most companies seem to be moving to separate compensation from career planning, if not in time, then certainly in focus. There is a sweeping trend toward opening up the appraisal process and involving the employee in meaningful dialogue. Some systems use a process of negotiation in an attempt to establish objective criteria that satisfy employees and supervisors. While automatic review by higher levels of management is built into only a few systems, there is some movement toward recognizing the need for mechanisms of redress. Some experts in the field feel that without this, vast numbers of people in the society are being deprived of due process.

While there are many opportunities for training and continuing education in American companies, age data are hard to find. Two programs in this section document successful retraining programs for older workers. One upgraded the skills of older electronics engineers at GE's Aerospace Electronic Systems Department while the other is turning machinists into skilled tool and die makers at the International Silver Company.

Occupational Alcoholism Programming, the third topic in this section, is just starting to become part of corporate and government personnel practices. The mid-seventies saw a big jump in the number of such programs, which managers are beginning to see as cost effective when they successfully correct poor performance due to heavy drinking. There is growing agreement among personnel directors that the threat of job loss is perhaps the most effective weapon against this disease. The high cure rate at the State Department, for example, may be due to the fact that the employee's job is put on the line early in the counseling process.

Preretirement counseling is another relatively new personnel responsibility. While many organizations are just starting programs and are, therefore, working with these age groups closest to retirement, those who have been involved for several years are moving toward initiating their retirement planning not later than age 55. Many enlightened personnel directors see the need to tie preretirement to career life planning in general. Employees want as much information as possible, particularly about financial entitlements, so that they can make intelligent choices.

Contents

YOUNG PROGRAMS
FOR OLDER WORKERS

1
New Work Arrangements

A number of new working arrangements have begun to appear in the marketplace in response to changing economic conditions. Novel ideas concerning part-time work and its emerging first cousin, phased retirement, as well as refreshing approaches to second-career training are considered in this section.

Traditionally, the part-time worker in America has been at the bottom of the economic barrel, a second-class citizen without job security, benefits, career paths, or status. Now inflation, unemployment, a longer working life, and the slower pace of economic growth are combining to alter this conventional view. Public- and private-sector initiatives have begun to appear which regularize part-time employment and provide career opportunities and benefits similar to those enjoyed by full-time workers, thus tapping people who, for a variety of reasons, prefer to work part time. This is happening in spite of labor union objections to permanent part-time employment, which can be summarized as follows: (1) part-time employment increases competition for jobs during periods of high unemployment, when many people who require full-time earnings are jobless; (2) increased part-time employment opportunities for some will blunt the drive for shorter workweeks for all; (3) part-time jobs are often at the lowest level, with insufficient pay and poor benefits; and (4) part-time employees may be hard to organize because their principal life interest lies outside their jobs. Nevertheless, some local unions have taken the initiative in organizing part-time units and they have succeeded in improving the working conditions of these units.

Northern Natural Gas Company's proposed change in status for part-time workers is a particularly comprehensive private-sector program. The revision of pension rules adopted in California and Kansas for teachers and other public employees represents a major breakthrough that permits the sharing of work in a shrinking profession. The California plan allows part-time employees of the public schools and the state university system to receive their full pension rights and benefit accumulation plus salary after the age of 50. In the San Francisco school district alone, almost 500

1

teachers are taking advantage of this situation, with consequent savings to the district of several million dollars over a five-year period. In Kansas, the 1979 changes in law that permit public school employees to receive both pension and salary are too new to evaluate, but officials expect a rush to job sharing. In essence, these programs are forms of phased retirement. They differ from the industry programs described here in that they pay out salary and pension simultaneously and can run for as long as 15 years. The plan in effect at the Wrigley Company phases out employees in three years, with reduced salary. Wrigley's trades off this salary reduction against an increase in pension benefits of about 8 percent a year. The Towle program phases employees out over the final four months of the retirement year with full salary and no reduction in pension benefits.

The second-career training options present a number of innovative models, from IBM's three-year-old retirement education assistance plan, to the efforts of New Career Opportunities, Inc., to teach annuitants how to start their own home-based business. The most elaborate program, a fully funded government plan offered to disqualified air traffic controllers, is a good model which achieved disappointing results, largely because of poor implementation by the Federal Aviation Administration, lack of adequate professional staff, insufficient screening of participants, inadequate counseling, and inattention to the age factor.

Part-Time Employment

NORTHERN NATURAL GAS COMPANY

Equality for Part-Timers

This total energy company is 50 years old. While gas is its principal product, Northern Natural is also involved in the exploration, production, and delivery of coal, petrochemicals, liquid fuels, and propane, as well as in a series of retail outlets for plastic products. A total work force of 11,000 is spread throughout 26 states, from locations with as few as one or two people to major plants with 1200 employees. Headquartered in

Omaha, Nebraska, the main office employs 1600 people. Annual sales are $2.5 billion.

Concern over declining productivity and escalating production costs has prompted top management at Northern to consider a new personnel policy in the area of part-time employment. Surveys which indicate that growing numbers of people would opt for part-time work if it were career related, permanent, and carried the same benefits as full-time employment, helped to bring the program into focus. According to Brooke E. Brewer, Northern's general manager of personnel resources, the target population for part-time work includes workers nearing retirement who want to decrease their schedules, retired people who wish to remain active, individuals combining school and employment, handicapped people who can work only a limited time span, employees who have reached a career plateau and want to develop outside interests and/or a second career, low-income workers who can increase their total salary with two part-time jobs, those who would otherwise be laid off during periods of recession and temporary cutbacks, people who are family oriented and want to spend more time with their children, and anyone who has sufficient outside activities and low enough economic needs to manage with a part-time income.

Brewer, a strong advocate of regularizing part-time employment and author of the current proposal, says he is 95 percent certain of approval. He lists the following advantages for the company: improvement in recruiting, because part-time work opens the marketplace to a large number of people who either cannot or will not work full time; increased job opportunities for minorities and students, which help the company meet its affirmative action goals; reduction of overtime and, thus, costs, because salary and benefits for part-time workers cost less than current overtime; extension of service hours to the public through the use of part-time employees for extra weekday hours and on weekends; reduction in turnover and absenteeism; the potential for increased productivity based on studies showing that part-time employees work at a faster-than-standard pace due to lack of fatigue, and based on increased productivity rates of employees in shared-job situations.

Brewer recognizes potential problems and disadvantages but believes they "can be minimized or avoided through well-designed programs." One possible difficulty is the lack of continuity, particularly in job-sharing situations, where tasks begun by one worker must be completed by another. Continuity can be provided by the supervisor, or by allotting a specific time for the two individuals sharing a job to confer on a regular basis. Brewer has solved this problem in his own unit, where he has one clerical position shared by two workers, working five hours per day each, with a one-hour overlap. This job is occupied by two employees who put in a total of 48 to 56 hours weekly, depending on business volume, and is described by Brewer as a "successful experiment." He anticipates that there will be at least one shared job in every department in the company within two to four years. While job sharing lends itself particularly to office work, there are many positions within the company that could be handled on a part-time schedule. Any job that is discrete and independent, with short time cycles, is appropriate, and these exist in maintenance, production, and technical areas. Seasonal part-time work is also possible, particularly in propane, where personnel are needed nine months a year.

A second problem concerns overcoming the second-class status that part-time employees have had in the past, based on their reputation as casual, undependable, temporary, and uncommitted workers. The only way around this, in Brewer's opinion, is to consider part-time employees on an equal basis with full-timers, that is, as permanent employees with the same access to benefits, skilled jobs, and career opportunities. Brewer predicts that, given this equality, more competent people will accept part-time jobs in the coming years.

Increased costs will occur in two areas—training and benefits. The former will be higher where two employees must be trained for one job and where more supervisory and classroom time is needed for on-the-job training. Actual cost projections will depend on the number of part-timers hired under the new proposal. But in the benefits areas, based on the 154 permanent part-time employees now working for Northern Natural Gas, the projected cost to the company is $100,000 annually if it picks up the entire tab, and half that much if it adopts a shared-cost plan. Since all Northern permanent part-timers now work more than 1000 hours per year, they are participating in the pension and trusteed investment plans. Additional benefits would include employee and dependent medical insurance, postretirement spouse benefit, noncontributory life insurance, salary continuance, long-term disability plan, tuition reimbursement, and vacation.

MACY'S

Large Part-Time Work Force Serves Special Groups

More than half of the 16,000 employees of Macy's New York,* which comprises 15 retail stores and 3 furniture outlets in the New York metropolitan area and suburbs, are part-timers. Their work schedules provide a degree of flexibility that is vital to the company and that also serves the special interests of a number of groups of employees, particularly women with families, retirees, and students.

Unlike organizations in most other industries, retail organizations are strongly dependent on part-time employees, particularly in the retail sales force. There are two traditional reasons for this: First, retail stores are open for much longer hours than could be covered by any full-time work schedule. (Most Macy's stores are open from 58 to 70 hours a week.) Second, salespeople must handle an uneven flow of customers. Heavy periods now include lunch and dinner hours, some evenings, Saturdays, and Sundays. And when customer traffic is heaviest, the sales force must be augmented.

Macy's suburban stores are open six nights a week (including Saturday) and, since September 1976, five hours on Sundays. To cover the Sunday staff needs, Macy's offered its employees the chance to swap one workday during the week for Sunday. However, the largest share of the work force needed for these extra hours has been filled by new hires; they are part-timers who work either Saturdays and Sundays, or Sundays plus two or three evenings per week. In the process of expansion, Macy's has recruited a good mixture of part-time employees: a larger-than-average number of males and an even larger group of females, especially young mothers with preschoolers or school-age children.

Thus, part-time work is more than a tradition at Macy's. It is a growing trend.

Two Types of Part-Time Employees

Macy's employs two different types of part-timers: middle-of-the-day employees and short-hour employees. Although they reflect rather differ-

*Reprinted from *Training and Jobs Programs in Action* by David Robison (New York: Committee for Economic Development in cooperation with Work in America Institute, Inc., 1978), pp. 195-199.

ent working groups, they have certain characteristics in common. They are people who prefer not to work a full schedule or to work during conventional working hours, or they are people who have been unable to find full-time work with regular hours.

Together, the two groups total more than 8000 or over half of the work force in the Macy's New York division, which constitutes roughly half of the company. Presumably, the same proportions apply among Macy's workers elsewhere. At present, Macy's has more employees on short-hour schedules than on middle-of-the-day schedules. In the past, the proportions were about equal, but the addition of the Sunday hours tipped the balance toward short-hour employees.

Middle-of-the-day employees work five fixed days a week, usually from 12 Noon to 5 P.M. on four days and from 1 to 9 P.M. on the fifth day. Others may work five mornings or five evenings, but those schedules are not typical. Thus, middle-of-the-day people regularly work between 25 and 28 hours per week. Wage rates and benefits received by middle-of-the-day workers are identical to those of full-time employees. They are relatively well paid for retailing employees. The entry-level wage is $3.40 per hour, and eight labor grades and an array of occupations are available to them. Some raises are based on merit; others are given according to automatic step rates. The benefits package includes a health plan and a pension after 20 years. Part-timers must work 1000 hours per year, or 20 hours per week, in order to qualify for a pension, as mandated by the Employee Retirement Income Security Act of 1974 (the federal pension law).

Short-hour employees work fewer than five days and often under 20 hours per week. They are mainly students, retirees, and moonlighters; that is, they are typically the very young and the older workers, though this group is much younger than the work force as a whole, and more of its members are male (although females still predominate).

The short-hour work force is not so stable as the middle-of-the-day group. Because students and retirees enter and leave the work force more frequently, the rate of turnover is higher. The wage rates are essentially the same as those paid to full-time employees, but because of their much shorter service, short-hour workers usually do not reach the higher wage brackets. Their fringe benefits are also more limited because many work at other jobs and receive benefits from their primary employer or are students who are covered by their parents' insurance policies.

Union Objections

Unions have often been unfriendly to the growing use of part-time workers. Union leaders have pointed out that benefits for part-timers are not always prorated, that part-timers may not have a strong commitment to union membership, and that it is often more difficult for a work force that is a mixture of full-time and part-time employees to agree on common negotiating goals if they have somewhat different interests and benefits.

Such union sensitivities affect Macy's as much as they do other retail chains, even though all part-time employees in these unionized Macy's New York stores (6 of the 15) are union members.

Exceptionally Stable Full-Time Work Force

Despite Macy's New York's increasing use of part-timers, its older full-time employees have proved to be an extraordinarily stable work force. There are 8000 to 9000 of them, and more than 1200 (one-seventh of the full-time work force) have at least 25 years of service with the company.

Gertrude G. Michelson, previously senior vice-president for personnel, explains why the company believes that the older work force is so stable: "Many of them came to work for us in the years shortly after the depression, when job mobility was so much lower. Also, there is the incentive in that our personnel policies are skewed toward long service; the benefits grow over the years. The personal lives of these employees have often been linked to the business. For example, they may have met spouses here, or their children may have been (or may now be) short-hour employees. These people take pride in staying with us. Such conditions don't apply nearly so much to younger employees."

A Tool for Retirement

Except in the case of its executive employees, Macy's imposes no mandatory retirement age. Therefore, part-time work is used by many employees as a means to stay on with the company and adjust to retirement. Some first-line supervisors have also asked to stay on a short-hour schedule. If management feels that they can handle the job, they are given short-hour jobs as appropriate work becomes available.

How many employees stay on past age 64? Although up-to-date

statistics are not available, Michelson says that "lots of people have availed themselves of the opportunity. But they usually don't stay at it very long. After a year or two, they often find that they enjoy staying at home more than they thought they would or that they can get along without the attachment to the store. But it is important in transition. It has tremendous emotional value."

Benefits

Older workers, housewives reentering the work force, students, and retirees all seem to be finding part-time employment eminently suited to their needs. Perhaps the largest group of part-timers is made up of women with very young and school-age children.

Macy's reports advantages to the company as well. The use of part-time employees offers the stores a better mix of males and females because it brings a greater number of younger males into an industry that has had a heavy over-representation of women, particularly in sales. Furthermore the efficiency of using part-timers has been most fully developed in retailing. As Michelson points out, retailing, like many other fields that use part-timers, has a basic work load, but it also has regular and predictable peaks and valleys in the volume and timing of the total work load during which part-timers can be put to highly productive use.

Society as a whole also gains because many groups, such as students, retirees, and housewives, who traditionally have higher unemployment and lower work force participation rates, receive income through part-time work and thus become more productive, contributing citizens.

WOODWARD AND LOTHROP
BULLOCK'S DEPARTMENT STORE

Older Workers Prefer Midday Hours

Generally, large retailers rely heavily on part-time workers. Woodward and Lothrop, with 14 department stores in downtown Washington, D.C., and the surrounding suburban areas, has a work force of 9000 employees, 7000 of whom work part time. Frederick Thompson, manager of personnel services, finds that annuitants are particularly valuable workers who "bring a wealth of life experience to their second careers," and, therefore, has been seeking them out for over ten years through the Retired Teachers Association, the Montgomery County Over-Sixties Club, and the Non-Profit Placement Service in Alexandria, Virginia. Thompson recruits for the Christmas season, getting anywhere between 20 and 40 people each year, and notes that about half of these recruits stay on in part-time slots for the rest of the year or longer. He uses older workers in sales and clerical positions, in the store's finance division, and says that grandmothers are particularly effective in selling children's clothing. Thompson observes that most older workers prefer midday schedules and choose to work from 10 A.M. to 3 P.M., avoiding rush hour and nighttime travel.

Diana Holland, manager of personnel relations for Bullock's Department Stores, concurs, pointing out that many older workers choose the 10 A.M. to 3 P.M. or 12 Noon to 5 P.M. slots. Bullocks employs 9000 people at their 22 stores in California and Arizona. The part-time work force numbers about 3500. Regular part-timers have set schedules and store assignments, work at least 18 hours per week (and as many as 40 during the Christmas season), and receive fringe benefits such as a 20 percent store discount, paid vacations, medical insurance, and membership in the company's profit-sharing plan, which is their pension vehicle.

THE TORO COMPANY

A Growing Business May Increase Benefits to Attract More Part-Timers

Toro makes lawn mowers, snow throwers, and other home maintenance equipment. This Minneapolis firm has experienced rapid growth in the last two years, more than doubling its 1977 gross of $151 million to $350 million in 1979. Correspondingly, its work force has grown to 4200 employees.

Toro has two categories of part-timers, permanent and in-house overload employees. The former work between 16 and 40 hours per week and have fixed jobs and responsibilities. They are eligible to participate in the company's profit-sharing plan if they work at least 1000 hours annually in each of the two years of the waiting period. Vacation benefits accrue during a 12-month period at the rate of one day of paid vacation for each 200 hours worked. These workers are eligible to receive full benefit of the company's new and used equipment purchase plan after completing 1000 hours. There are two kinds of in-house overload workers: on-call employees and those on regular schedules. On-call employees have no limit on the number of hours they can work, while those on regular schedules put in less than 16 hours per week. The former receive the same benefit package as permanent part-time employees.

While part-timers at Toro constitute only a fraction of the total work force (1½ percent), Eric Browning-Larsen, corporate benefits analyst, says that the company is considering the addition of medical and life insurance to the benefits package to attract more of them. Recently he has observed a trickle of workers in their sixties applying for part-time positions, mostly in the clerical area. Toro also will make every effort to adjust the schedule of any full-time employee who requests reduced hours for medical reasons, depending on job responsibilities. At present there are six or seven older manufacturing workers who are employed three days a week.

SAN FRANCISCO UNIFIED SCHOOL DISTRICT

New Pension Rules Make Part-Time Work Viable

A major breakthrough in job sharing and part-time employment in California became possible with the passage of legislation in 1974 permitting part-time employees of the public schools and the state university system to have their retirement benefits based on their previous full-time employment. In 1976 the Board of Education of the San Francisco Unified School District approved three plans which combine increased incentives for early retirement with part-time employment. Together these plans have made it financially feasible for almost 500 teachers to accept part-time work. It is estimated that savings to the district will exceed several million dollars over a five-year period.

The first two provisions are limited to employees over 50. The third is open to all certified teachers.

Plan A is known as the Early Retirement Consultant Plan. Here any teacher over 50 who has taught for ten consecutive years in the state (the last five must be in the San Francisco District) can retire, receive a full pension, and be hired as a consultant for duties other than classroom teaching. These include curriculum development, special studies, training of new teachers, development of organizational skills, general administration, and office work. Consultants are paid $150 a day and can work a limited number of days each year on a decreasing scale. Up to age 55 the limit is 50 days a year, at 56 it drops to 43 days, at 57 to 37, and so on until full retirement. In practice this means that a 55-year-old annuitant with a pension of $9000 a year can earn another $7500 by working the maximum number of days. Consultant contracts run for five years, or up to age 65, whichever comes first, and can be cancelled as of July 1st of each subsequent year. The plan has been received enthusiastically by the teaching staff, with 400 employees currently enrolled in the program.

Plan B was devised for those who wish to continue teaching on a half-time basis without reduction of fringe benefits. With this approach, all teachers over 55 who earned at least $16,280 on the 1975-76 salary scale and have ten years of service with the district can work 50 percent of the time required by the previous year's assignment in mutually agreed upon activities. These include classroom teaching as well as a host of support possibilities, such as resource teaching, in-service training, advising on classroom management or curricula. Sixteen teachers have opted for this plan and are working on a variety of schedules which include half-a-year, half-day or a three- and two-day split on alternate weeks. While their actual salaries range between $9140 and $11,000, their pension contributions are calculated as though they were working full time and earning full salary. Most have elected to stay in the classroom.

The same situation is true of Plan C, which is open to all certified teachers in the district. Here partnership teaching at half pay still permits benefits to be calculated on the full-time salary that goes with the job. Sixty-four teachers of all ages have combined under this plan, and several pairs match a more experienced teacher with a younger one. One older teacher chose this plan so that she would have time to care for an ill parent. A husband and wife are each sharing a separate job and dividing their parenting responsibilities as well. According to Robert Seymour, director of personnel, many more teachers had signed up for this option but were laid off when the district reduced its teaching staff by 1200 employees, the combined result of declining enrollments and Proposition 13.

WICHITA PUBLIC SCHOOLS

Pension Plus Salary

New incentives for job sharing are being tried in Wichita, Kansas. Here

2872 teachers instruct 46,000 students in 102 schools. Only 132 teachers, or about 4½ percent of the work force, work part time. Twenty of these part-timers are sharing jobs on the elementary level under a recent Board of Education policy which accepts teacher-initiated job-sharing proposals and allows participating teachers to determine how they will divide teaching tasks, schedule their time, and communicate with each other and the rest of the school staff. These employees receive one-half of their base pay in salary; other benefits and teaching credits are computed on their half-time status. More than one-third of the part-time teaching staff is over 40, as are 7 of the 20 job sharers.

But Robert D. Wright, director of employment relations, is excited about the possible effects of certain changes in the Kansas Public Employees Retirement System (KPERS) law in 1978. KPERS amended its rules at that time to permit employees to retire at age 60 or over, receive their pensions, and be rehired into their existing jobs or into another job for which they are qualified. In the summer of 1979, the Wichita School Board guaranteed such reemployment after retirement, providing that application is made by the end of August of each year. While only one supervisory employee heard about this change in time to apply in 1979, Wright expects a rush to job sharing once the news is widely known. He points out that under this enabling legislation a 60-year-old teacher earning $15,000 a year, who might not have been interested in sharing a job because he or she could not survive on $7500, can now collect a pension of $7000 along with half a salary for a total of $14,500. Wright, who is enthusiastic about job sharing both as a way to employ more teachers and to improve the quality of teaching situations, envisions pairing older instructors with younger ones. That way more experienced teachers can provide younger colleagues with valuable on-the-job training.

Phased Retirement

THE WRIGLEY COMPANY

Phased Retirement—An Old Option at Wrigley

Although phased retirement may sound like a new concept, it is not. According to William Frank, assistant treasurer of the Chicago-based Wrigley Company, his firm has been offering it as an option "as long as anyone can remember." Wrigley's management believes it is important to allow its 6000 employees an opportunity to get used to retirement gradually if they so desire. They permit anyone who stays until the company's normal retirement age of 65 the choice of taking one month off without pay the first year, two months the second year, and three the third year, compensating personnel for the reduced income with an increased pension. Since the pension benefit is based on earnings between ages 62 and 65, phasing does not reduce the basic benefit but increases it by eight percent. If the pension would have been $100 per month at 65, it is $108 at 66, and $117 at 67. The maximum would be $147 at age 70.

Wrigley, which sells $500 million worth of chewing gum each year, typically retires about 50 employees annually. They are split between those who take early retirement at 55 (with actuarially reduced benefits) and those who work to 65. About 19 people stay beyond 65, but 60 to 70 percent of these work only to the end of the year to get a generous group incentive payment. Of the dozen employees who continue to work, six to eight choose phased retirement; the rest work full time for full salary but earn no additional pension credits.

TOWLE SILVER COMPANY

Thirty Years' Experience With Phased Retirement

This small manufacturer of sterling flatware has built phasing into its retirement process since the early forties. According to Clifford Marshall, personnel manager, Towle was the first company in the country to include the idea in its personnel policies. The thrust came from top management, says Marshall, who is pleased someone "up there" recognized that people are "scared stiff" of retirement. "It is the greatest thing our people have. They start off worrying about what they will do with their time, and end up anxious for their retirement date so that they can get on with all the things they want to do.''

Towle's program gives the potential annuitant 40 paid days off during the four months prior to retirement, one day a week during the first month, two during the second month, three in the third month, and so on. By the month before retirement the employee has fewer work days than free ones. The program applies to all employees retiring at age 65 and is included in Towle's contract with the International Jewelry Workers.

Eleven employees have retired annually during the last four years, many of them around 60, in spite of a reduction in pension benefits. Only one clerical worker has elected to remain beyond 65. Employees use their 40 free days to catch up on repairs around the house, get used to the full-time companionship of their spouses, and become involved in volunteer activities.

NEW ENGLAND MUTUAL LIFE INSURANCE COMPANY

More Paid Vacation—A Kind of Phasing

New England Mutual Life Insurance Company, a Boston-based firm with 2600 employees, gives extra paid preretirement vacation time to employees with at least ten years of full-time employment. They receive two additional weeks vacation in the year of their sixty-second birthday, three weeks in the year of their sixty-third birthday, and four weeks in the year of their sixty-fourth birthday. While they must take the additional vacation during the calendar year in which it is given, they can defer and accumulate some but not all of their regular vacation time. In practice many employees end up with 30 to 50 days of paid vacation coming to them at the time of retirement.

Retirement becomes effective on the first of the month following the decision to retire. If employees have accumulated vacation time, they can either be paid for it in a lump sum or extend their retirement date until the accumulated vacation is used up.

Cheryl Montalto, assistant director of employee services, says that 56 percent of those who retire do so between the ages of 60 and 64; the rest leave at 65. In 1979 two employees stayed beyond age 65 and worked until the end of the year. Of those workers who have accumulated vacation, it is a 50-50 tossup whether they take the time or the money when they retire.

GORDON E. McCALLUM AND ENGINEERING-SCIENCE

Gordon E. McCallum is a senior vice-president in charge of liaison for Engineering-Science, an international consulting firm in the environmental field with 600 employees and 15 officers. McCallum joined Engineering-Science in 1966 after 30 years with the Public Health Service and a short stint at General American Transportation Company. Although the company's headquarters are in Arcadia, California, McCallum is based at the Washington, D.C., office, which he opened several years ago.

Last year the company's president decided to try phased retirement, using McCallum as a "guinea pig, I guess because of my age." McCallum is 74.

The plan is simple: McCallum is on a reduced schedule, three-quarter time in 1979, half time in 1980. His salary is based on the same rate he earned when working full time, but prorated for the shorter workweek. The firm's pension plan is contributory, and payments are figured on current reduced earnings. McCallum does not participate in other benefits since he is covered from his previous employment. "I don't really have to work, I like to work," he says.

IBM

A Variety of Career Shifts

IBM, the fifth largest industrial corporation in the nation, is a full employment company with a work force of over 190,000 in the United States. Strong sales volume growth averaging 14.6 percent since 1964 has made the commitment to full employment possible. The philosophy behind it is simple and pragmatic; if people are secure in their jobs, they will be more flexible in making the changes IBM asks of them.

Since 1970, more than 17,000 IBM employees have assumed new job responsibilities as a result of rebalancing efforts, and of these, over 7000 were retrained. Helping to manage these substantial shifts is the responsibility of the Corporate Resource Group at IBM headquarters in Armonk, New York. During periods of unbalanced work loads, the group reviews staffing projections from the divisions and aids in balancing workload and employee resource by referring those units with excess employees to those with openings. Where major shifts have occurred, as in 1971-72, the company has occasionally posted notices of career opportunities on bulletin boards, described them at employee meetings, or had company representatives encourage requests for transfers. When an employee move was required, IBM paid for relocation expenses. According to the director of personnel resources, ''we try to move work to places where we have a surplus of people. If we can't do that, we move people to the work.''

These changes have led to a variety of second careers within the company. Listed below are some examples of both total career shifts as well as career enhancements.

• Assemblers whose work disappeared due to technological developments or changes in business conditions have moved into clerical jobs and received nearly three months of course work in areas such as typing, English, and office practices.

• Engineers have received the training necessary to successfully become computer programmers.

• Engineers, programmers, and administrative people in plants and laboratories have been moved into the marketing environment, both as sales representatives and systems engineers.

• Technicians and manufacturing employees have gained the skills necessary to transfer to the customer service area.

• A number of employees whose skills and experience were associated with the space program were moved to other parts of the business where they were given additional training in skill areas such as process engineering and materials science.

• Certain types of development and manufacturing engineers have taken part in a program which augments on-the-job training with a semester-length program at a university and allows them to become facilities engineers.

In all the areas listed above, employees are chosen based on their individual skills and qualifications as well as their expressed interest in the new career area. Employees of varying ages have participated in these programs. IBM has no program which either attempts to include or exclude employees for any reason based on demographical data, just as it has no special compensation or promotion programs for a specific group. Many employees who have taken up new careers like not only their jobs, but also the challenge in learning new tasks and the satisfaction involved in mastering a new and different job assignment.

Education Assistance for Retirement

IBM's three-year-old Retirement Education Assistance Plan provides potential retirees and their spouses with $2500 each in tuition aid starting three years before retirement eligibility and ending two years after retirement. The purpose of the plan is to help develop new interests and/or prepare for a second career. A wide variety of courses meet the intent of the program, including real estate, television and radio repair, interior decorating, creative writing, musical instruction, carpentry, photography, hotel management, and accounting.

In 1979, 1200 people completed their courses of study, 50 percent more than the previous year. While television, radio and motor repair, as well as real estate were the most popular areas, one IBM annuitant is now a tennis pro, having used the plan to attend tennis college. Another took voice lessons and is now singing professionally, while a third studied small business practice in preparation for opening his own picture framing shop. One became a gemologist after going to school in that specialty, and an information systems programmer who is three years away from retirement is studying Chinese cooking with the idea of giving lessons herself or starting a catering business.

NEW CAREER OPPORTUNITIES, INC.

Senior Achievement with a Capital $

For most people the energy crisis is a problem, but for Robert D. Jones it is turning out to be a blessing. Jones, an early retiree of the Pacific Telephone Company, has started his own, home-based business selling SWIM-WARM, a cream which permits the body to retain its heat and enables swimmers to dip into unheated pools and chilly oceans. SWIM-WARM looks so good to pool manufacturers these days that they are hailing its virtues with editorials in trade magazines such as *Pool and Spa News*. Why? They are afraid that people who cannot heat pools will not buy them. SWIM-WARM may be their salvation.

Jones originally developed the product for his personal use. A Pasadena resident, he likes year-round ocean swimming. But with winter water temperatures hovering around 57 degrees, long-range swimming is not feasible—thus his invention. When he retired, Jones thought it would be a simple matter to sell his cream to surfers. Had he followed that hunch, his might well have been one of those nine out of ten small businesses that fail every year. Surfers are not his market because SWIM-WARM makes one slippery. Jones is succeeding, however, in doubling his sales each month in his second year of operation, largely because of market research and other business techniques acquired at New Career Opportunities (NCO).

NCO is the brainchild of Clarence N. Parker, retired executive vice-president of Junior Achievement of Southern California, whose aim is to rescue "exiled adults" from unwanted retirement and teach them how to start small businesses. Originally funded by a grant from the Edna McConnell Clark Foundation, the nonprofit program established a model which combines the theoretical and practical, borrowing equally from the junior achievement format and Parker's experience in starting and successfully operating three businesses during the Great Depression. Each NCO class runs for seven weeks, meeting three hours a day, and accommodating an average of 23 people. Central to the training is the model corporation, which students establish, operate, and liquidate. Timed to the various stages of its development are presentations by volunteer business specialists from the world of finance, industry, and government, who give advice on capital, loans, taxes, market research, advertising, record keeping, sales, and accounting. There are workshops in goal setting and problem solving and discussions with successful small-scale entrepreneurs.

All of the corporations established in NCO classes have avoided bankruptcy and some have declared a 15 percent dividend, says Parker, who believes small business failure is caused by too much government regulation and not enough know-how. "We found that you must have a basic vocabulary and a knowledge of business problems before the Small Business Administration or college courses can do you much good."

NCO results are impressive: 163 adults (90 women, 73 men) have completed the training, and 83 percent were between 50 and 70 years old, with a median age of 55. Attendance was 84 percent, attrition only 9 percent. Students listed 34 previous occupations, and educational levels went all the way from high school to one Ph.D. Ninety-one were retired and 112 had incomes of $10,000 or more. Fifty-five percent are currently in business.

NCOers have gone into a wide variety of enterprises. A former engineer now operates a design and marketing business for his inventions—a food dehydrator, a water purifier, and a water still. A retired executive secretary started a secretarial service, and an ex-electrical worker developed a collapsible "book nook" which he sells to schools, colleges, and U.S. embassies overseas. A grieving widow went into business lithographing and marketing her artist-husband's best work. A former Lockheed manager has turned his woodworking talents into a profitable doll-house business, and a retired civil engineer parlayed a flair for model boat design into a lucrative contract with a Japanese manufacturer, who intends to mass produce his radio-controlled boats. An ex-state employee who was reared by deaf parents is now a free-lance interpreter for the deaf in schools, courtrooms, and offices. One woman started a roommate-finding agency for senior citizens, another opened a tour service in Los Angeles, and a third has more business than she can handle reupholstering furniture.

The human benefits have been substantial. Participants have gained confidence, self-esteem, know-how, companionship, and hope. The group therapy aspect is important, according to the classroom coordinator of the pilot program.

"Retirement seems to hit men the hardest in our culture, and without work they seem very sad, lonely people. They miss being needed within their occupation," said Parker. "The problem with divorced and widowed women is different. There the trick is convincing them that the skills they brought to raising a family—mediating, planning, supervising—can be used to manage a small business. Most women simply are not aware of the managerial talents they have."

Parker's newest goal is to sell "senior achievement" to large corporations as an addition to their preretirement counseling programs. Lockheed has endorsed the program with a letter of support to the business community and is sponsoring an NCO class for its retirees. Hughes Aircraft, TRW, Rockwell International, and Pacific Telephone have shown "some interest," according to Parker.

Because foundation funding has ended, NCO will charge its corporate clients tuition of $100 per person. Ross Hopkins, Public Affairs Manager for Lockheed California, says the corporation wants to test the program's appeal on a fee basis. Parker concedes that NCO is not for everybody. Many students learn that their ideas are impractical. Most see the course as worthwhile. And Robert Jones insists that it was indispensible for him. "I can't get over how willing successful business people are to help others," he says. "I guess that's the American way. It's very encouraging."

THE AIR TRAFFIC CONTROLLERS

Stipends for Second-Career Training

The 1972 Public Law 92-297 established a second-career program for air traffic controllers. The legislation was developed in response to the 1970 Corson Report, which examined air controller functions from a wide variety of perspectives. It was found, that with the growing volume of air traffic, an increasing number of the 17,000 air traffic controllers in the United States were being removed from active duty because of rising levels of physical and psychological stress. The problem was how to deal with the air traffic controller who is trained intensively for one specific job but can no longer function at it.

The total second-career program, including the training portion, was an attempt to address this question. It was available to controllers who were medically disqualified or were unable to maintain the technical proficiency required for the job. The overwhelming percentage (90 percent) fell into the first category. This was not the only available option. Controllers could choose to retire under the civil service retirement system on a full annuity, or seek a partial annuity based on their disability. Or they could seek compensation from the Department of Labor, Office of Workers' Compensation Programs (OWCP), under the Federal Employee Compensation Act, if they believed their disability was job related.

According to David Trick, director of operations for the Professional Air Traffic Controllers Organization (PATCO), these latter choices have several drawbacks. Controllers' pensions are less than half their salaries. To be eligible for early retirement with a full annuity, a controller needs 25 years of service, or 20 years at age 50. As of May 1972, when the law was changed to permit early retirement, only two traffic controllers had met these specifications. Similarly, OWCP processing takes from 6 to 18 months, and the applicant must prove that the disability is job related. Although 60 percent of disqualified controllers apply, only 45 percent qualify for this type of help.

The Federal Aviation Administration (FAA) was charged with administering the second-career program, which began in 1973 and was terminated by Congress in October 1978. The government agreed to pay full salary and fringe benefits for up to two years, as well as all tuition and training costs. Vocational counseling and testing were also covered. Controllers were permitted to choose any legitimate training program that had a reasonable expectation of employment. The FAA had to approve the choice and the arrangement was formalized by contract, thus providing for joint accountability.

As of October 1978, 2500 air traffic controllers had participated in the program. Their average age was 45. When the program began in 1973, 62 percent of the participants entered academic fields, such as business administration, accounting, management, education, and public relations. Sixteen percent took technical or vocational training in areas such as photography, and 22 percent elected on-the-job training in real estate or retail sales; as small business contractors; or as carpenters, upholsterers, and mechanics. By 1977 this pattern had shifted, with 45 percent in academic disciplines, 20 percent in vocational-technical fields, and 33 percent pursuing on-the-job training (OJT). A much higher percentage was interested in the last category because the rate of employment among those electing this option was considerably higher than in the first two. But the overall placement rate was disappointingly low. The FAA says only 7 percent of the controllers in the program found employment in second careers. While PATCO questions the methods used to arrive at this figure, it admits that the program did not achieve an acceptable success rate.

Total expenditures were $104,465,238, 90 percent of which was for salaries. Training costs amounted to $4,387,540, and administration added another $453,000 to the bill.

The question is: why the low success rate? Was it the model, the execution, or a combination of both?

The FAA Analysis

Harold Alexander, national program manager of the FAA's Training Program Division, gives three major reasons for the poor placement rates. The first has to do with the controllers' age at the time of separation, their previous high salaries (in the $28,000 range), which led to unrealistic expectations regarding future earnings, and their faulty perceptions of themselves and the job market.

The second relates to other available benefit programs, which functioned as disincentives. For example, disability retirement provides an income of $12,000 a year, while OWCP recipients receive 75 percent of their final salary plus up to four years of training, all of it as tax-free income.

Finally, according to Alexander, the controllers possessed limited skills which were not easily transferable. Generally they were high school graduates who had difficulty handling the academic requirements of the degree programs they chose; on the other hand, they resented trainee situations, which they saw as geared to youngsters in their twenties, not to 40-year-old males with 20-year career histories.

The Union Position

David Trick sums up PATCO's opinion: "The second-career program of the air traffic controllers was a great idea that was maladministered to death." Trick charges that the agency failed to train controllers for alternate positions in the FAA or other branches of government that were related to their original careers and to which they could bring their previous talents and skills. By suitable work, the union means training future controllers, devising new air traffic control systems, conducting air traffic surveys, or performing personnel work with current controllers. Of those who went through the second-career program, only two individuals were offered government jobs.

Trick criticizes the agency for inadequate screening of program participants, some of whom had severe emotional problems and were not able to make reasoned career choices. He claims that the vocational aptitude testing that was promised was haphazard and, when it was administered, was handled by FAA personnel staff rather than by professional job counselors. He insists that since the FAA had to approve the programs selected by the controllers, they bear as much responsibility for "unrealistic choices" and he claims that the agency was "insensitive" to union complaints during the life of the program.

An Objective Judgment

Michael D. Batten, senior staff associate at the National Manpower Institute in Washington, D.C., believes that the age factor was not given sufficient attention in the FAA program. Pointing out that the length of unemployment periods are consistently greater for older job seekers than for their younger counterparts, Batten suggests that air traffic controllers should start preparing for second careers much earlier than they do now, so that they will be ready for the transition. He goes on to say that there are parallels between the air traffic controller model and other high-technology organizations and that some important lessons can be drawn from the experience of the air controllers in order to avoid obsolescence among engineers. He suggests more flexible occupational structures which would allow engineers and senior research personnel to move into other careers within their own agencies. "Performance appraisal systems can serve as one indicator that a career change may be called for. More age-directed use of opinion research surveys could tap job-change aspirations well in advance of confrontations over performance downturn." Batten recommends that employers "cost out" second-career options and asks, "Is it better to provide some investment in a second-career program or sustain a less productive employee until he or she drifts off into retirement?"

Successful Placements

Despite the critiques and charges, there were successful individual experiences. One controller combined regular accounting courses with on-the-job training and got an excellent job with an accounting firm. Another used his OJT with a major airline to become a public relations executive in the same company. Several made the switch into teaching and one high school instructor got a B.S. in education. One became a respiration therapy technician and another an environmental engineer. One went to agriculture school and became a farmer; another got an M.S. in agriculture. Several became successful mechanics, one became a paralegal assistant, and two became nurserymen. One group of controllers entered a community college which agreed to give them 60 hours of credit for their former training. This allowed them to complete their degrees during the two-year time limit allowed by the program. Several retrained as X-ray technicians. Quite a few successful controllers did well in the real estate and sales area. These are people-oriented jobs which depend on effective communication, a functional strength of the controller's former training. And one got an aviation-related job as a mechanic in an aircraft frame factory.

AEROSPACE CORPORATION

Early Retirement for What?

Early retirement is still in vogue in the aerospace industry, where the average retirement age hovers somewhere between 57 and 60. In 1978 the Aerospace Corporation carried out an early retirement assistance plan limited to six months for any vested professional employee with ten years of service, offering severance pay equal to one week's pay for each year of service plus a bridge payment of $375 a month for up to 48 months, or until age 62, whichever came first. The plan was instituted partly in response to the desire of older employees to retire, and partly in response to the need of opening up promotion opportunities for younger staff members. Seventy-six individuals—20 administrators and 56 technical people—took advantage of it.

Aerospace is a not-for-profit corporation established in 1960 by the United States Air Force for its Space and Missiles Systems Organization. Located in Los Angeles, the corporation employs a highly sophisticated staff of 3500, half of whom are management and technical people. There are more than 400 Ph.D.s on staff and many more individuals with master's degrees in two disciplines, as for example, math and engineering or chemistry and physics. The corporation designs complete space and missiles systems, advises the air force on letting contracts to build them, and provides the necessary program-management function to run them.

The personnel department did a follow-up study of the 1976 annuitants which revealed that the 39 individuals who actually retired were, at ages

58 to 62, the older members of the cohort. Of the remaining 37, nine took immediate, full-time jobs as engineers with pay equal to or slightly higher than their exit salaries. Four of these remained in the Los Angeles area, two went to Boeing in the northwest, one to Washington, D.C., and the other two to Southern California.

Five became real estate salesmen. All of them had prepared for this second career by taking courses while they were still at Aerospace. They were thus able to use the income bridge to get established. Three went to nonmilitary organizations, two as administrators of a school district and a professional engineering society respectively. The third went to work for the state civil service as an electrical engineer in contracting, an occupation that is quite different from electrical engineering in the space industry. He was able to adapt his basic education through self-study.

The remaining 20 went into business for themselves. Five became building contractors, using their engineering background and supplementing it with self-study or courses given by the extension service of UCLA. All five got building contractor licenses. Two, a mathematician and a physicist who were married to each other, went to New Mexico to raise a special breed of horses, elevating a hobby to a full-time business. One took over the management of a print shop he had bought some years before with an eye towards retirement, another opened an antique shop in Idaho, and a third, an optical engineer, became a licensed optometrist. One started a machine shop, another a gift store. One engineer, who had helped a relative with the design of bakery equipment years before, brushed up on the recent technology in the field and went to work selling this equipment. A corporate lawyer opened a private practice, while a manager took over the avocado ranch he had purchased eight years earlier.

The survey prompted management to investigate the possibility of regularizing second-career preparation through a formal funded program. A feasibility study conducted in 1979, which queried older employees about their interests and opinions of the value of such a program and possible ways of funding it, was expected to lead to recommendations for a second-career program by mid-1980. That plan has now been shelved because a turnaround of business has made it necessary not only to retain people but to hire annuitants.

YALE UNIVERSITY

Professors May Retire, but They Do Not Stop Working

Yale's mandatory retirement age of 68, established in 1903, will remain in force until 1982, when the exemption granted to educational institutions under ADEA expires and the academic community joins the rest of the nation in accepting 70 as the new retirement age. A recent look at the status of Yale professors emeriti reported on 19 of the more than 180 professors holding emeritus status. If they are any indication, the majority of Yale professors emeriti go right on working.

Only 3 of the 19 have actually retired. The rest are teaching, writing, and consulting. All are traveling. Seven are or have been visiting professors at other universities. Ten have been writing on production schedules that range from a book every other year to several multivolume works. One is busy with his own minifarm and two national forestry organizations. Another was a founding faculty member of the School of International Service at American University in Washington, D.C., and taught in Tokyo on a Fulbright fellowship. An ex-law professor serves as chairman of the Connecticut State Labor Relations Board, which has turned out to be a full-time job. A history professor, with his wife, preceded Alex Haley by spending several years researching her family's genealogy. And one is busy writing articles about the unconstitutionality of compulsory retirement at any age.

Job Redesign

TEKTRONIX, INC.

Creative Retention

Helen Thomas is 69 years old and works as a medical placement specialist with Tektronix, a manufacturer of oscilloscopes and display instruments. Founded in 1946, Tektronix has grown into the largest private employer in the state of Oregon. Although its work force of

20,000 is young, there is a group of about 25 long-service employees who have been with the company since it started. It is with these workers that Helen Thomas has done some innovative job redesign.

Job redesign usually means reorganizing a department or an entire unit so that employees will have responsibility for planning, setting up, and checking their own work. Its aim is to increase worker satisfaction and eliminate the fragmentation that is associated with mass production techniques. As Frederick Taylor's "scientific management" theories sought to remove decision making and responsibility from the worker's life in the nineteenth century, so job redesign is trying to put them back.

A successful European example of this type of activity took place at the Volvo plant in Kalmar, Sweden, where teams of workers replaced the traditional automotive production line. In this country, both AT&T and the Prudential Life Insurance Company are involved in redesigning work with an eye toward more efficient organizations and greater job satisfaction.

Helen Thomas's interest is pragmatic. She wants to help workers retain their jobs despite physical limitations caused by aging or accidents.

Before taking on her present situation at the age of 65, Thomas had worked as manager of safety and health at Tektronix for 16 years. She supervised four first-aid stations, ran health education programs, and referred people with health problems for medical treatment. During that time she got to know the employees, the physicians who treated them, and the detailed requirements of most production jobs. This experience uniquely qualified her for her current position, which involves helping employees who are receiving workers' compensation or other forms of salary continuance to get back to work.

Thomas has successfully redesigned jobs for older workers with residual physical limitations. For example, a carpenter who sustained a back injury was not able to bend. He could still manage the saws and lathes, but could not flex his back to reach and trim molding. This part of his job was deleted and picked up by others in the carpentry shop, while he was given the added function of driving a truck and delivering supplies.

In another situation, an assembler who sits at a bench could not flex his neck muscles and look down. Thomas had a styrofoam easel constructed that contained the controls the assembler had to reach so that he could look straight ahead while working. Similarly, an audit inspector in her forties spent her days turning knobs and testing instrumentation, which meant she had to hold her arms up for long periods of time. Over the years she had developed a condition in which a spur under the collar bone compresses nerves and vessels. When she held her arms up continuously they would become numb from lack of blood. Thomas had all her controls put at lap level so that her workbench resembled an airplane cockpit. With this accommodation, blood circulation was not impaired and she could continue to function productively.

Thomas has also had wooden foot rests installed, or has had the height of chairs, tables and benches redesigned to relieve tension on the legs and lower back, a condition which intensifies with aging.

Where the job cannot be adjusted to the worker's physical condition, Thomas arranges for transfer. Some older workers have developed tendonitis after years of using clippers and screw drivers. They have been moved to clerical jobs in production departments where their knowledge of parts' numbers allows them to check IBM runs. Others who cannot sit or stand for long periods but who can still lift have gone to the warehouse where they can do stock work and packing. One 58-year-old woman who was in production planning and scheduling, a job of some physical stress involving selecting components and testing them for technical accuracy, could not continue after undergoing open-heart surgery. She was re-trained in modification processing.

Thomas herself is not sure when she'll retire, if ever. "You see," she says, "I like to work."

2
Reentry Workers

Reentry workers are generally women who have left the work force for varying periods of time, usually to raise a family, and have returned to the labor market. Their collective presence as wage earners constitutes a major social revolution. Currently, 40 percent of the nation's workers are women.

Although it is true that many women are working, it is also true that they occupy positions of lower status and pay than men. The Conference Board's 1979 study of corporate efforts to improve the status of women notes that in both male- and female-intensive industries, men occupy most of the high-level managerial positions. The same report cautions that, even with the best intentions, it will take several decades to correct this imbalance. And champions of the women's movement continue to decry the fact that women, on average, earn only 57 percent of the amount that men earn.

These facts indicate that women need a great deal of help in improving their employment opportunities. This section deals with several attempts to provide that help. The American Woman's Economic Development Corporation was established with government funding after a woman went to the U.S. Department of Commerce with statistics which showed that only 4.6 percent of all small businesses in the United States were owned by women. The career facilitation programs sponsored by the National Science Foundation and funded by the Congress also grew out of the significant underrepresentation of women scientists and engineers in the fields for which they were trained. Their successful results—with 65 percent of the participants employed and another 10 percent in graduate school full-time—indicate that this retraining model could serve to upgrade the skills of both men and women in high-technology industries, where rapid change and early obsolescence are common.

Similarly, the legislation to provide help for displaced homemakers is a response to the enormous dislocation caused by the high divorce rate, the breakdown of the traditional American family structure, and the continued inflation which makes two paychecks essential. A look at the numbers indicates that the programs in place represent a mere beginning. One hundred displaced homemaker centers and $5 million of CETA funding are hardly a sufficient response to the needs of the 4 million displaced homemakers around the nation. It is clear that greater efforts by both the public and private sector are needed.

AMERICAN WOMAN'S ECONOMIC DEVELOPMENT CORPORATION

The Distaff Side of Small Business

After 20 years as a travel agent, Shirlee A. Rousseau bought Paramount Travel Service in 1973 from the retiring owner. At that time Paramount's clientele was 40 percent corporate and 60 percent vacationers. In spite of her long experience, the owner had serious problems as a result of the 1974 recession and the subsequent inflation. Rousseau attended 16 hours of seminars run by the American Woman's Economic Development Corporation (AWED) in 1977. What she learned made her realize she would have to switch emphasis and "stomp the streets for corporate business." By 1979 the client mix had changed to 70 percent corporate and 30 percent vacationers, with gross sales of $1.8 million and a net of 8 percent.

The seminars Rousseau attended were part of the initial pilot program run by AWED, the first federally funded, nonprofit organization in the country to provide entrepreneurial women with comprehensive training and technical assistance. The corporation came into being when Beatrice A. Fitzpatrick approached the Office of Technical Assistance, Economic Development Administration, U.S. Department of Commerce. She was armed with figures which showed that only 4.6 percent of small American businesses were owned by women. In October 1976, a grant of $124,000 was awarded to establish a model program in New York City that would be offered free-of-charge to women applicants who were considering starting a business from scratch, or who were already owners of their own businesses and were having difficulty maintaining them. Fitzpatrick became executive director of the program.

AWED now offers two kinds of service. The first is a free, year-long mini-MBA program consisting of 20 evening seminars supplemented by six "brainstorming" sessions, in which each woman's business is analyzed and critiqued; a one- or two-day on-site business audit by an experienced management analyst; a review of the participant's business plan; assistance from volunteer business advisors and counselors in special areas of need; and regular contact and evaluation of progress by a marketing expert and management analyst assigned to each group of approximately 30 women.

A 1979 survey of business owners testified to the success of the program. Current figures, compared with those of the year before the participants entered the program, showed that net sales increased by over $17 million, 893 jobs were retained, 450 new jobs were created, and 75 percent of the businesses had expanded or diversified. There was a direct relationship between the length of time a woman stayed in the program and the growth of her net sales volume.

In June 1978, AWED started a free counseling service, available to women planning to start a business who needed feedback on the feasibility of their ideas, and to women already in business who had specific problems. Funded by the Small Business Administration (SBA), it matches clients with business experts who are knowledgeable in the entrepreneur's area of need. Over 3000 women have been seen in individual sessions averaging one and a half hours each; with the addition of more volunteer counselors in late 1979, AWED had the capability of assisting 150 women each week.

Participants in the early peer training groups, who received instruction from an interdisciplinary staff recruited principally from the Harvard, Wharton, and New York University business schools, helped identify the most prevalent needs—"management education and technical assistance." For this reason, much of the training emphasizes proper capitalization, a well-defined business plan, a sales development program, accounting procedures, banking relationships, merchandising, marketing, promotion, personnel, and overall management. While the business topics covered today in the year-long program remain similar, the curriculum has become more structured. It is constantly evaluated and innovations are introduced as new needs are recognized. Because of their ability to combine theory with practical experience, seminar leaders are now drawn from the business world. Members of the Young Presidents' Organization, executives of large corporations and small businesses, "role models" as well as AWED's accomplished, professional staff, now address the training of women entrepreneurs.

Variety is the spice of business life at AWED, and women of all ages, races, and backgrounds have come for help. Their businesses cover a full spectrum—from catering and designing knitwear to selling ice cream and plumbing supplies. Lately, however, the kind of applicant has changed. "We used to get only women who had started their own businesses, but now we're getting widows, almost all of whom had been advised by their husbands' counselors not to keep the business—and all of whom had decided to do it anyway," says Fitzpatrick. "I would say it's part of the whole movement toward financial independence."

One such woman is Martha Koenig, president of Natale Building & Contracting, Inc., whose nontraditional career began when her husband, a master plumber, went bankrupt 17 years ago. She helped him put the firm back together, becoming a full partner with authority to make decisions in the areas of administration and management. After Nathan Koenig died, his wife decided to take over the whole operation, going to **AWED for training in advertising, selling, and financing.** Helen Wacey used the money her husband left her to create a retail center called Scarborough Fair in Seagirt, New Jersey. With help from AWED, Wacey has managed to build a thriving concern. And Roslyn Rosenblatt is managing her husband's locksmith and automotive lock supplies firm in spite of the fact that it is "definitely a man's business. I had trouble with some accounts who felt they could take advantage of a woman and not pay," she said recently. "I sued them. I won."

CAREER FACILITATION PROGRAMS OF THE
NATIONAL SCIENCE FOUNDATION

Scouting for Scientists

In 1976 the Congress directed the National Science Foundation (NSF) to "develop and test methods of increasing the flow of women into careers in science." To carry out this mandate, NSF tried several approaches, one of which was directed to women with science degrees who were not making use of their training. A preliminary study by the Denver Research Institute (DRI) revealed that while there were about 900,000 women with undergraduate degrees in math and science across the nation, they were vastly underrepresented in the scientific work force, university faculties, and in professional societies. For example, only 0.9 percent of the members of the American Institute of Chemical Engineers are women. Almost half (47 percent) of all women with degrees in math and science were "unemployed and not seeking" employment in 1974. This was in contrast to 12 percent of the men holding such degrees (*Women and Minorities in Science and Engineering*. Washington, D.C.: National Science Foundation, 1978). Of the 6000 programs of continuing education for women surveyed by DRI, none were directed at post-baccalaureate women scientists, mathematicians, and engineers.

To correct this imbalance and utilize the wasted talent represented by the unemployment or underemployment of these women, the National Science Foundation funded 21 Career Facilitation Projects (CFP) in 12 states and the District of Columbia. Since 1976, slightly more than 1000 women have participated in CFPs in the fields of electrical, chemical, and environmental health engineering, chemistry, biochemistry, polymer science, computer science, and interdisciplinary programs which cut across these divisions. Twenty-seven percent of the participants were over 40.

A detailed evaluation of the programs conducted by the Denver Research Institute in 1979 catalogued the following results:

● Across the board, 65 percent of the participants were employed, another 10 percent were in full-time graduate school, and one-third were both working and attending school.

● The majority of the employed women were earning between $10,000 and $20,000 annually in private industry. An average per-participant investment of $2600 in federal money produced this result, money which will be repaid in additional taxes. Thus the projects appear to be cost effective.

● The most successful programs were in areas where there is a demand for skilled employees, such as engineering and computer science.

● Participants with the greatest need for employment were the ones who got jobs. Other considerations, such as previous experience, were not as significant.

● Actual cost per participant varied greatly from project to project, depending on a number of factors, such as length of training period. The amount spent did not relate at all to the successful completion of the programs.

• There is a demand for this type of training among participants and potential employers. Carol Shaw, assistant dean of engineering at the University of Dayton, where programs in electrical and chemical engineering have been held, says she is called regularly by personnel officers of Fortune 500 companies who are looking for qualified candidates. General Electric hired eight graduates of Dayton's first program in 1978.

• Enthusiastic response from science educators and employers, and interest among potential participants indicate that some form of scientific retraining will be continued at many of the universities that have been involved in the program.

• The two reasons most frequently given by the 25 percent of the sample who dropped out were (1) current employment, and (2) the presence of children under 14, both of which conflicted with school.

• In a Denver Research Institute survey, scientific and engineering employers who had hired reentry women scientists indicated that women scientists are generally perceived as stable, career-oriented, and having a desire to achieve. Thus, a ripple effect may help other employed or job-seeking female scientists.

Science career facilitation projects are open to women who have received at least a bachelor's degree in math, science, or engineering at least two years before their acceptance as participants. They have been of three main types. In the first type, participants are updated in their original fields. In the second, they are converted from one field to another, as for example, from chemistry to chemical engineering. In the third, skills in the participant's original field are upgraded and training in a new field is added, giving the participant the equivalent of a special interdisciplinary degree.

The Polytechnic Institute of New York conducted two career facilitation programs in polymer science during the 1977-78 and 1978-79 academic years respectively. Polymer science includes all materials involving large molecules, such as plastics and synthetics. Because of Polytechnic's proximity to the tristate area of New York, Connecticut, and New Jersey, where the chemical industry is concentrated, Polytechnic has always provided excellent placement opportunities.

The initial group consisted of 33 women, five of whom were over 40; 58 percent completed the program. The second group consisted of 30 participants, eight of whom were over 40; 80 percent completed the program. Bernard J. Bulkin, dean of arts and sciences, explained that the markedly improved success rate the second time around had to do with better screening and a wider pool of applicants. An increased number of older women were attracted to the second group because the program no longer required applicants to have earned their undergraduate degree within the past 15 years.

The program offered short courses, audio-tape workbook courses, special seminars, regular Polytechnic courses, and counseling and placement services. An individualized approach worked particularly well, allowing those participants who were employed a substantial degree of self-scheduling. Frequent exams gradually accustomed reentry students to the rigors of academic work. Grades were high, mostly A or B. Although 54 percent of the first group were unemployed when the program started, most had worked in the past, usually not as chemists, but most often as lab technicians. The inability to find work or to earn an adequate income were the reasons most often cited for applying to the program. Perhaps that is why one of the most popular special seminars was in résumé writing and interviewing.

At the end of the first year, 14 of the 19 who completed the program were considered to have upgraded their jobs—by moving from being unemployed to having a job as a chemist; by changing from a nonchemistry job to one in the field; or by getting a raise in pay or more supervisory responsibilities in an existing chemistry job. Seven who had been unemployed found jobs as chemists. For example, one woman who had been an instructor in a nursing school that closed got a good job with the Oakite Corporation shortly after enrolling in the program. She later moved to a higher supervisory position with Lederle and sent two of her technicians to Polytechnic's second NSF Women in Science program. Two other women went to work with small venture-capital type companies on Long Island, one of which is developing a new material for soft contact lenses. Several participants became college instructors.

A year later, 17 of the 19 were contacted. Eleven were working full time, all but one as research chemists, college professors, or chemical engineers. Four had received their master's degrees in polymer science, and all of them had scored very high grades. Only two were not working. One had just quit her job as a chemist to start her own business, while the other was having a baby, after which she planned to return to graduate school. It is interesting to note that while only one-third of the original group had planned to attend graduate school, by the end of the program nearly three-fourths of the women had decided to try for advanced degrees.

Among the 14 dropouts in the first group, the largest portion were women who were accepted but never appeared, indicating a lack of serious interest. Three others found the commuting too difficult, two could not handle the demands of their current jobs and the program, three found the material too difficult, and one said that the program did not meet her specific needs.

Displaced Homemakers

As a legal entity, displaced homemakers have only a four-year history. Pioneering legislation in California, Maryland, and Florida to fund displaced homemaker centers was passed in 1976. In 1978 the Congress amended the Comprehensive Employment and Training Act (CETA) authorizing $5 million for displaced homemaker programs. By the end of 1979 there were over 100 centers throughout the country, and 26 additional states had passed legislation recognizing the special counseling, training, and referral needs of women whose major career has been unpaid labor within the home.

Displaced homemakers are people who have provided services for their families for a substantial period of time and who, in their middle and late years, are forced into the labor market by the sudden loss of income due to divorce, abandonment, death, or the disability of a spouse. Many have difficulty securing employment because they lack marketplace skills. Furthermore, unless they are 62 and have been married for more than ten years, they are not eligible for Social Security from their spouses' accounts, nor are they covered by unemployment insurance.

Advocates for the displaced homemaker movement are pleased with the CETA amendments, but they point out that by using this vehicle Congress has limited aid to those who meet the near-poverty level CETA eligibility requirements. Statistics indicate that the problem is larger than the available remedies. Tish Sommers and Laurie Shields, founders of the Older Woman's League Educational Fund (OWLEF), an advocacy organization working for legislative change, point out that there are presently 4 million displaced homemakers in the United States and that 3 million of them are between the ages of 40 and 64. With one-third of all marriages ending in divorce, and alimony awarded to only 14 percent of divorced women; with the number of widows topping 12 million, and 47 percent of all women over 65 living on less than $2000 a year, the need for assistance to displaced homemakers is immense.

NEW YORK STATE DISPLACED HOMEMAKER PROGRAM

New York has established centers in the western part of the state, New York City, Rockland, and Nassau counties which form a statewide network. Receipt of a one-year, $1 million grant from the Department of Labor in April 1979 has provided funding for individual and group counseling, job placement, education and skills training, referrals, workshops, conferences, newsletters, and information about health, finances, and the law. There is no income limitation for the New York program, according to Louise Finney, assistant industrial commissioner for the state, who notes, ''This isn't an expensive program. The whole goal is to make these women self-sufficient.'' Of the nearly 1000 women served in the Buffalo pilot program, 87 percent of those registered for an intensive job-readiness program were successfully placed in jobs or training at a cost of $675 per placement. These placements and other counseling provided under the program resulted in a total of 150 homemakers placed in jobs and 50 others enrolled in skills training. Jobs were in a variety of occupations— programming or servicing computers, or as clerks, typists, secretaries, administrative assistants, paramedics, nurses, and counselors.

A skills training and supportive services program contract signed with the New York City Department of Employment, and funded by CETA Titles IIB and III, together with a linkage between the Displaced Homemaker Program and the Private Industry Council of New York, is expected to provide another 245 jobs and training opportunities during 1980. Carol G. Durst, coordinator of the New York State program, estimates that by the end of the first year, 10,000 women will have been reached throughout the state, 1000 with individual counseling, another 800 in group counseling, 5000 through one-shot workshops, and the rest via conferences and newsletters.

In New York City four agencies comprise the DHP consortium. Each functions with a paid staff of three, 50 percent of whom are displaced homemakers themselves. At one of the Brooklyn Centers operated by Women in Self-Help (WISH), codirector Estelle Fonseca explains that referrals to other agencies have made it possible for the small staff to handle 50 women a month since June 1979. Business schools and adult education courses at local high schools provide training for participants, who receive a minimum wage while attending classes. For placement, WISH uses the New York State Employment Service, private agencies like Mature Temps, or a computer which lists all available job openings at the other Brooklyn center.

Fonseca observes that most of the women are in their forties and fifties and prefer training in business skills rather than nontraditional jobs. They are getting entry-level positions as typists, bookkeepers, stenographers, file clerks, and secretaries. Placement rates at WISH run about 75 percent.

A form of OJT that is becoming increasingly popular is the unpaid internship. Carol Durst's assistant for the first nine months of 1979 was a displaced homemaker in her fifties who had been out of the work force for more than ten years. Her duties included developing a mailing list, research and resource acquisition for a statewide conference held in June 1979, telephoning, correspondence, and record keeping. She was so good at her job that she obtained a paid position as an administrative assistant in a real estate firm, where she functions as office manager. She has gone on to get her real estate license.

CENTER FOR CONTINUING EDUCATION FOR WOMEN, VALENCIA COMMUNITY COLLEGE, ORLANDO, FLORIDA

In April 1977 this center established a structured 70-hour program for displaced homemakers called Building for Success, which is the equivalent of five college credits. The curriculum covers personal coping styles, assessment of employable skills, short- and long-term goals, and assertiveness and skills training. Upon completion, participants enroll in a job club and begin their job search. Here they learn how to locate available jobs, write résumés, and conduct successful interviews.

Some 550 women have taken part in the program, and 75 percent of them have found entry- or higher-level jobs in four major employment categories—clerical, hotel-motel, child care, and sales. The average participant is 45 years old and has a strong tendency towards traditional employment.

For those women not ready for so intensive a course, a second model was developed in 1978. It covers the same curriculum developed in eight three-hour seminars. This model seems to attract women with slightly higher educational levels. Two who had master's degrees got good jobs in mid-1979, one as an administrative assistant with the Florida Banking Association, the second as a management trainee with the Hyatt Corporation.

THE MARYLAND CENTER FOR DISPLACED HOMEMAKERS

This center, the second such operation to be established in the nation, is operated under the auspices of New Directions for Women, Inc., located in Baltimore, Maryland. It offers a wide variety of counseling, training, and placement services. In August 1977, under the aegis of its Small Business Project, the center began an Independent Cleaning Contractor (ICC) training program for displaced homemakers interested in operating their own small businesses.

The ICC project consists of 75 hours of classroom and on-the-job training (OJT) over a three-week period and is designed to teach participants professional team cleaning skills and basic business management. Topics include planning, marketing, publicity, record keeping, bookkeeping, contracting, and dealing with customers as home-cleaning contractors rather than as "maids" or "domestics." According to Diana McLaughlin, coordinator of the Small Business Project, this is an ideal kind of enterprise for displaced homemakers because it does not require large capital or inventory and is home based. The fine art of estimating and simple repair of cleaning machines are also part of the curriculum.

The first ICC project began with eight persons who started their own businesses. A feature article in the Baltimore *Sun* brought 3000 phone calls from potential customers, and the businesses were instant successes. Each has not only survived the crucial first two years in business, but has expanded its staff from two to four women. Owners report that they are grossing from $17,000 to $25,000 a year. Contracts are usually for one year and provide for two cleanings a month at an average charge of $35. Team cleaning allows two women to cover three homes or apartments each day. Customers are of three main types—bachelors, single-parent families, and women who have returned to work. The success of the first round prompted the center to repeat the course in 1978 and another four businesses have been launched.

PROJECT RE-ENTRY OF THE CAREER AND VOLUNTEER SERVICE, CIVIC CENTER AND CLEARING HOUSE, INC., BOSTON

The internship concept is the centerpiece of this privately funded tuition program designed to help women into the labor market. Over its five-year history, Project Re-entry has developed internships with more than 75 businesses and nonprofit organizations in the Boston area for 120 participants, 78 percent of whom have found paying jobs.

The program follows the normal academic year and combines six weeks of workshops with a seven-month internship of at least 20 hours per week. Internships have been held in public relations at the United Way of Massachusetts; in curriculum planning at the Boston Center for Adult Education; in counseling and placement at Radcliffe College; in public relations at the Boston Transit Authority; in hospital work at the Massachusetts Department of Training; and with the Tri-Lateral Council, the Licensed Practical Nurses Association, Dunkin' Doughnuts, Digital Company, and the Shawmut Bank. Some of the program's graduates are now providing internships for current students, thanks to a manual published by the Civic Center and Clearing House, and Project Re-entry has been replicated at Drake University in Iowa, Columbia University in New York, and the state volunteer office in Anchorage, Alaska.

Originally started with a $3000 private gift and $7500 from Permanent Charities of Boston, Project Re-entry has been self-supporting since its inception. Tuition charges, which began at $325 for the year, are now $750 per participant.

3
Secondary Organizations

The 1979 Harris study of American attitudes toward retirement found that 46 percent of current annuitants would prefer to be working, and that 48 percent of employees between the ages of 50 and 64 intend to extend their working life. These figures reflect a number of social and economic conditions, of which inflation is only one, though probably the most important. No group is harder hit than those who are trying to survive on fixed incomes. Other factors include the better health and education of today's retirees, making them able and willing to work, and the shortages which are beginning to appear in the labor market, specifically in high-technology fields and clerical and secretarial functions. The problem is matching available skills with existing jobs. Harold Adams, vice-president and executive director of Retirement Jobs, Inc., points out that "retirees form the largest pool of untapped experience in the country, and both business leaders and private citizens are now accepting this fact."

Statistics indicate that Adams is right. Mature Temps, a nationwide employment agency which provides older-worker services to its client companies, experienced a 20 percent jump in volume in 1979 over the previous year, and Senior Personnel Employment Council (SPEC) of Westchester County, New York, processed 33 percent more applications in 1979 than in 1978. The Second Careers Program in Los Angeles reports that more annuitants are seeking paid employment and observes that they represent a broad spectrum of talents—secretarial, clerical, managerial, academic, and technical. Second Careers is now faced with the task of producing a data bank for paid employment similar to the one they have created for volunteer jobs. This matching problem is widespread. Robert Custer, director of retiree relations at Sun Oil, says his biggest problem, since inviting retirees to come back to work, is establishing a data bank of annuitant skills to fill the hundreds of temporary jobs that occur in his company each year (*See also* Chapter 5, The New

"New-Hires," Sun Company). In this connection, American companies might consider borrowing from Daniel Knowles' experiences and constructing data banks of annuitant talents by industry, occupation, skill, and geographic location (*See also* Chapter 6, Performance Appraisal, Grumman Aerospace Corp.).

The productivity of older workers, and employers' consequent satisfaction with them, is a point that cannot be overstressed. Richard Ross, president of Mature Temps, says that older workers, as a whole, have fewer problems than any other age group and that his clients find hiring them to be cost effective. A parade of personnel directors have repeated this theme in the hundreds of interviews that were conducted to collect data for this volume. Business need, rather than good intentions, is, of course, the quickest way to open up jobs for older workers. SPEC's 1979 experience in Westchester County should not be overlooked. After 25 years of not being able to place their clients with any of the large corporations in the area, the SPEC staff suddenly found jobs for six retired individuals with two major corporate employers last year. This surely reflects the changing demographics of the county, where 20 percent of the population is now over 60.

Perhaps the most encouraging news for older workers is the placement and retention rate achieved by individuals over 50 who were clients of Job Finders, a West Coast agency that specializes in self-directed job placement. The 95.6 percent placement figure needs to be put in bold face and underlined. It proves that a self-directed job placement program which gives its clients hard and specific information about the private sector, puts the responsibility of the job search squarely on the individual, and reserves for the staff the role of enabler, produces an extraordinarily high rate of success.

JOB FINDERS

Magic Numbers

Job Finders is a three-week workshop in self-directed placement designed to infuse the job-search process with private-sector efficiency. A nontraditional approach to securing employment which shifts the emphasis from the agency to the participant, Job Finders is self-help with a capital S. Program Director Dick Wright says, "We teach job applicants to dazzle employers and meet private-sector expectations.'' Wright and a staff of six, all with backgrounds in both private and public employment, are dazzling more than employers with placement rates in the private sector of 76 percent for public service employees completing one year of training under the Comprehensive Employment and Training Act (CETA). Since a 1977 study showed a previous private-sector placement rate of 24 percent for CETA workers, Job Finders becomes a program worth studying in depth. More compelling are the placement rates of CETA workers over the age of 50, which stand at 95.6 percent. The question is, what is the magic?

The Background

Job Finders is a child of Proposition 13. Located in San Mateo, California, whose total work force of 294,300 people included 1567 in public-service employment (PSE), Job Finders was originally conceived to serve two groups. The first was the large contingent of expected CETA lay-offs who could not get employment in local government because of a "bumping" system, which prohibited them from taking the jobs of regular employees "cut" because of the lack of local funding. The second were PSE employees approaching the end of their one year of CETA eligibility. The latter, known as regular entry participants, spend the final three weeks of their CETA year at Job Finders, an attendance that is mandatory if they want to receive their last three weeks of pay. It is interesting to note that one-third of this group, which includes people of all ages, obtained unsubsidized employment within three weeks after entering the Job Finders workshop, while the 76 percent placement rate took six weeks to achieve.

There are two other routes into Job Finders. Early entry participants are workers who ask to attend the workshop after three months of PSE and stay only for the first week of orientation. They then go back to their subsidized employment and spend the next nine months looking for a job in the private sector, using Job Finders' techniques. Here too clients' ages are across-the-board. Although statistics in this category are not conclusive until the end of the fiscal year because they build with the passage of time, as of July 1979 they stood at 54 percent.

Direct entry was initiated in the spring of 1979. Job Finders' staff took a hard look at PSE participants and concluded that public-service employment would not have been needed at all had they been able to sell skills they already possessed in a competitive manner. They began accepting these workers, who also receive a minimum hourly wage stipend for the duration of the workshop. As of October 1979, these participants had a placement rate of 91 percent in jobs with salaries that averaged $4.55 an hour. This population included groups identified as hard-to-place—the handicapped, aged, displaced homemakers, ex-offenders, single-parent heads of household. Overall, Job Finders served 520 people in 1978. It achieved placement 80 percent of the time in entry-level positions averaging $4.92 an hour.

According to Jan Bourdon, Job Search Supervisor, the 20 percent who fail include people who become ill or move out of the area. The remainder are individuals who are just not ready to work.

Job Finders operates in a professional setting that has a corporate look to allow clients to understand what is expected of them in the real world of business. The most modern equipment and reference materials are used. Attendance, punctuality, and proper dress codes are stressed. Start-up costs were $25,000, out of the first year's budget of $197,597.

The Workshop

The program is geared to handle 16 clients per week. The first week is devoted to orientation, the next two to the actual job search. Wright emphasizes that the methods taught can be used for the rest of the participant's professional life. The aim is to deal with past failures openly, to analyze what has gone wrong before, to handle anger, frustration, and the loss or lack of self-esteem, and to help participants come to grips with their own skill levels, and understand how they fit into the actual job market. Day one is crucial. Wright promises that the program will make the participants competitive, and that by noon they will know more about themselves and job-search techniques than they thought was possible. The method used is the employment application, which each participant fills out at once. A line-by-line analysis identifies inaccuracies, gaps in information, damaging evidence, and reasons for previous terminations. The most troublesome section is the one devoted to past employment history. Clients are required to obtain current, accurate information for this section, using local telephone books, and are told to include the names of all supervisors, even those unlikely to be favorable. They then call their ex-bosses and ask if they can be counted on for a good reference. Where the situation is hopeless, the job is eliminated from the application but usually this does not happen. The staff does not intervene unless it is absolutely necessary. One such case involved a 35-year-old truck driver who had been fired after 15 years from his only job because he was caught pilfering merchandise. Since it is impossible to explain away a 15-year employment gap, the staff called the president of the company and asked him to stop blackballing the worker. They promised to keep track of the man in exchange for a positive recommendation. He got a job and so far has stayed out of trouble.

The application analysis provides a form of instant skills identification. Objectives are also defined at this point, and while clients often start off with unrealistic goals, they soon catch on to the idea of starting where they are and using one job to get a better one.

Day two begins with résumé development. The staff teaches the rudiments, the clients write their own résumés which the résumé specialist helps them edit and refine. Once typed, one copy goes into the file as the permanent record. It is updated after placement in case clients want to change jobs. This is a long-range administrative service provided by Job Finders.

Job objectives are next. Each client lists three desired jobs and puts a list of skills possessed under each one. The rest of day two is spent interviewing, with the staff role-playing the employer's part. These interviews, which are filmed, effectively simulate the tough pressures of the actual meeting.

On day three the interviews are played back on a 5-foot screen and watched by participants and staff, who rate and discuss them. All reactions are collected and the interviews are graded on a curve. Says Wright, "These tapes tell the whole story. It is the first time any of them have ever had an idea why they failed." Where an interview is an absolute disaster, it is repeated privately. The participants, armed with a mental catalogue of their mistakes, as well as the criticisms, comments, and suggestions of their peers and the staff, go home and practice. "The second round of interviews shows the progress," says Wright. "Once they know what is wrong they really work on this."

The fourth day is devoted to research. Participants write two job descriptions, one ideal, the other realistic. They list under each ten skills they have and ten that they need. This helps the job-search staff identify areas which the participants must work on when they enter the job-search portion of the workshop. Reference materials on hand include the *California Dictionary of Occupation Titles,* three vocational guides and *Contacts Influential,* considered by the staff the best source of information for their particular needs because all firms are listed by industry code, area code, phone prefix, and zip code. This information is vital in an area where public transportation is poor, and clients, aiming for the most part at entry-level jobs, cannot afford extensive travel to get to work. With the use of these research materials, clients can locate businesses in areas they can reach and list them for future reference. Similar guides are available in all regions. Information about them can be secured from Standard and Poor's or Dun and Bradstreet.

On the fifth day clients refine job-search techniques. The state employment service is eliminated because it keeps jobs that have been filled on file for several weeks. Want ads are considered the best source of information; 60 percent of all job possibilities are found there. Participants get a short course in how to read want ads and the various headings under which the same job can be listed. They bring their own newspapers, from which they cut out and paste all job possibilities, creating a customized job-search list. Another method of locating openings is the "cold call." This means calling companies in given locations and asking if they have any jobs available. The staff demonstrates various "cold call" scenarios and the clients write out "cold call" dialogues for later use. Wright labels this approach "private sector moxie." The possible rejection factor is handled by telling clients they can hang up. This "out" acts as a safety valve and allows participants to try the technique. A survey by the staff in July 1979 showed that 12 participants generated 14 interviews from "cold calls" in a three-week period. Each client averaged 50 "cold calls" during the second two weeks of the workshop. If the "cold calls" do not generate the specific jobs that the clients are seeking, they are told to ask if the firm has any openings. This information is fed to Jan Bourdon, who either finds a suitable candidate or calls the firm, asking permission to make a proper professional referral.

The Job-Search Room

This area contains a large square table, 16 phones and chairs, portable cubicles for privacy, and all reference tools—want ads, the Yellow Pages, employment directories, phone interview scripts, "cold call" dialogues, résumés, lists of typical questions employers ask, form letters (that confirm appointments, thank employers for information and interviews), and road maps. Everyone gets on the phone. There is a mix of age, sex and race and a lot of teamwork occurs, with participants giving each other advice and support. People with cars offer others rides. There is immediate feedback via the motivation board, where all job interviews are listed and marked with blue stars, and all hirings are posted. This is when participants learn time management, decision making, and problem solving. They must keep accurate records of all calls and results; this also helps to establish an automatic job bank. Each client is expected to set a minimum daily goal. The staff is careful at this juncture to respect the difference between guidance and dependence. While they identify individual problems, the approach is to help clients find ways of improving their own methods.

There is a practice room where participants can sharpen their skills. They can improve reading and math levels, practice on typewriters, dictating and 10-key machines. An employer board lists all businesses with on-going hiring, and an employers' information file contains material about companies with job descriptions and sample applications. An answering service takes calls for clients and these are posted on an information board so that employers can get back to job seekers.

Results

Results are monitored by a Stanford University Ph.D. candidate and his staff. Retention rates for all participants are 93.6 percent at 30 days; 81.1 percent at 90 days; and 81.2 percent at 180 days. Wright says, "We have driven the monitors wild because we teach the philosophy of changing jobs if the firm is not fulfilling employee development obligations or things are not as they seemed when the job was offered. Many of our participants have followed our advice and we suspect that the statistics could be revised upwards."

Numbers do not tell the whole story. Since Job Finders preaches quality placement it allows clients to turn down jobs deemed unsuitable, so they may continue searching for one they really want. The following list is a cross-section of jobs obtained by CETA workers over age 50 between July 1978 and July 1979. Fifty people were involved, 30 men and 20 women; 27 men and 19 women got jobs, for a placement rate of 94 percent. The 90-day retention total was 26 men and 18 women.

Type of Position	Employing Firm
Production Scheduler	Dalmo Victor (Div. Textron)
Secretary	Professional Standards Board
Mag Card Operator	Metal Fabricators
Statistical Typist	Stanford Research Institute
Maintenance Worker	Peninsula Maintenance
Security Guard Supervisor	Security 86
Receptionist	Vacu Blast Corporation
Recruiter	American Sportsman
File clerk	Grover Easterly Mahl, Inc.
General Office	House of Non-Ferrous Metals
Property Management	Select Investment
Mechanical Maintenance	Christian Candle Co.
Sales Representative	Ad Mark Corporation
Carpenter-Painter	K. Smith Corporation
Warehouse Worker	Taylor Sales, Inc.
Child Care	State Licensed Home Child Care
Instructor	Menlo College
Electronics Specialist	C & W Communication
Home Care Provider	Visiting Nurses Assn.
Order Desk	Peninsula Office Supply
Security Guard	California Plant Protection
Personnel Coordinator	Quality Care
Woodworker	Hileys Creation
Job Developer	State of California
Diesel Mechanic	Bayside Equipment
Mechanical Assembler	Beckman Instruments
Janitor	Geno's Janitorial
Electron Assembler	GTE Lenkurt

Mr. R. Cooper, manager of marketing services for Vacu Blast Corporation, says that the job applicants he has interviewed from Job Finders have all been outstanding. His firm has hired eight of them and 75 percent have stayed in their jobs. Cooper says he had to sell his company on the first applicant because of an inherently anti-CETA attitude. She was, however, an exceptional candidate who is still with the firm and has helped convince management to hire other CETA people. His advice to job developers: send your best candidate to new firms to break the ice.

No one can put numbers on the human benefits of this program, except, perhaps, those who have found work through it. One 54-year-old white woman, a displaced homemaker who had been out of the job market for 22 years, got some filing and receptionist experience from her CETA employment. Although she considered her age a major obstacle, after attending Job Finders she secured a position in the general office of a large concern, where she can use her existing skills and develop new ones. Six months later her feeling of self-worth has greatly increased. Another woman, 61 years old and black, who had raised eight children (seven of whom have college degrees) was caring for economically disadvantaged children during her CETA experience. She entered Job Finders on September 25, 1978 and got a permanent job as a personnel coordinator with a private firm on October 4 of the same year. She is still there.

SECOND CAREERS PROGRAM

Placement Services Demand Grows With Inflation

When the Second Careers Program in Los Angeles was established in 1975 its purpose was threefold: to help Southern California companies initiate or expand their preretirement and retirement programs, to locate volunteer opportunities within the community, and to open up more paid second-career jobs for older persons. While its aims have not changed, inflationary pressures are emphasizing the paid employment aspect of its work. A 1979 survey of 113 job-seeking retirees indicated a wide variety of backgrounds and skills. The majority were secretaries and typists while the second largest group came from management—individuals who had been presidents, vice-presidents, and administrators before they retired. Other fields included accounting, real estate, banking, interior design, small business, and film editing. There were also ex-college professors and instructors in the group. Second Careers intends to match these retirees with job opportunities within the community and within their client companies, which include such large corporations as United

California Bank, Atlantic-Richfield Company, Security Pacific National Bank, and Prudential Insurance Company (Western home office).

The Second Careers Program was jointly conceived by the Edna McConnell Clark Foundation of New York, which funded it until 1978, and the Los Angeles Voluntary Action Center, which administers it. In 1974, a McKinsey and Company study was commissioned by the Clark Foundation to project the problems of retirement by the year 2000. The study reported that today's retirees are usually healthier, better educated, and more accustomed to high pressure, highly structured workdays than their predecessors were. It assumed that retirees will find it increasingly difficult to adjust to 40 or 50 additional leisure hours each week. Moreover, by the year 2000, retired people could account for up to one-third of the nation's total population. The prospect of a large group of retirees ready and willing to be active on either a paid or unpaid basis, prompted the funding of Second Careers.

The organization provides participating companies with the methods and personnel to support custom-designed retirement counseling. It provides special workshops, seminars, and a data bank of over 3000 social agencies that are receptive to using retired people, and 20,000 volunteer job opportunities in 2000 different categories.

Second Careers is a nonprofit organization which charges participating companies for its services. Fees range from $500 a year for membership, which includes consulting services, access to information, and meetings with retirees, to $1500 for complex analysis and program design. Second Careers will review a checklist of possible organizational activities and evaluate the company's demographics, past and present retiree activities, projected staff time, and corporate policies for an upgraded retirement program.

In addition to assisting the large corporation it serves, the Second Careers program is helping smaller companies that want to become more active in retiree relations but lack the experience and staff time to do so. The program reaches out to retirees individually as well as through corporations. There is no charge to the retiree for any services. Thus Second Careers provides two significant programs—one for businesses concerned with improving their employee relationships and one for retirees. The ultimate goal is to encourage older persons to remain active and productive members of society.

MATURE TEMPS

The Business Approach to Employment Services

In 1979 Mature Temps provided jobs for 15,000 people over the age of 50 through its 14 offices around the country. This translates into $14 million worth of temporary employment services for its clients, which include insurance companies, banks, major oil companies, utilities, retail stores, and museums, and represents a growth rate of 20 percent over 1978's volume. "And," says Richard Ross, the 33-year-old president of Mature Temps, "we could have placed more. The demand for jobs exceeds our supply of workers."

Mature Temps is a subsidiary of the Colonial Penn Group, a corporation which has had a long involvement with older people through its connections with the American Association of Retired Persons and the National Retired Teachers Association. Mature Temps' largest office is in New York City. There are also offices in Boston, Philadelphia, Plymouth Meeting, Pa., Washington, D.C., Chicago, Dallas, Houston, Los Angeles, and San Francisco.

Most of the jobs filled by Mature Temps personnel are clerical and secretarial. There is also a demand for people in marketing research and mailroom work, as well as for receptionists and messengers. Wages run from $3.10 to $8 an hour and are competitive with other temporary employment services.

Mature Temps is not an employment agency; it is a service which hires workers directly, pays their wages, mandates employee taxes, workers' compensation, and disability insurance, and fills its clients' orders on a contractual basis. There is a direct employer–employee relationship. While there are no fringe benefits, it does offer referral bonuses to employees who refer friends who in turn work for Mature Temps. The company does its own screening and skills evaluations, checks references, and provides training in word processing and transcription typing. This service is free to applicants and there is no obligation on their part.

Ross reports that employers are particularly satisfied with the older workers provided by Mature Temps and says that, as a group, they generally have fewer problems than any other age category. "They're the ones who get to work when the weather is bad," he says. One bank recently told him that these workers are more productive than younger employees. "The result," he points out, "is that this group lowered their cost by giving greater productivity,"

Ross defines temporary jobs as working a full day or a full week for a variety of employers. A person might put in 30 to 50 weeks a year for many different concerns. Mature Temps also provides temporary workers on a more regular basis. It currently has two shifts of donation takers at a New York City museum, each shift working 4 hours a day, 5 days a week.

The work has tended to be mildly seasonal, with the greatest volume in the first calendar quarter. "Our shortest supply time is from August to November, when students go back to school and transients are seeking permanent jobs. We could provide more work opportunities during that period if we had more registrants," Ross adds.

OLDER AMERICANS EMPLOYMENT AND TRAINING CENTER

A Variety of Training Options

Older Americans Employment and Training Center (OAETC) was established in 1970 under the auspices of the Older Americans Organization. It is funded through CETA and has two primary purposes, advocacy for senior citizens and vocational skills training for those over 45.* Located in Fresno, California, the urban center of an agricultural area devoted to the grape and citrus industry, it serves a mixed population of white, black, and Mexican-Americans who are unemployed or underemployed. Referrals come from other social agencies, including the Department of Social Services, the Employment Development Commission (which is the California State Employment Service), the Commission on Aging, and the Fresno Employment and Training Commission (FETC). FETC is also the CETA prime sponsor.

From modest beginnings, when eight retired teachers decided they wanted to help senior citizens in the legislative area, OAETC has grown in stages. It received its first training grant in 1975 from the federal government for 35 people over the age of 55 and established two basic programs, home health aides and home and building maintenance. By

*The age was dropped to 45 with the restructuring of the OAETC program in October, 1978.

fiscal year 1977—78 OAETC was responsible for outreach, intake, orientation, referral, and training. Outreach provides some 400 senior citizens a year with information about available programs. Intake and referral are a means of funneling clients into either vocational training, OJT, or work experience. Orientation is used to explain the various options and to assess where each individual would find the best placement.

A total of 237 clients received training in 1977—78, 146 of them in six different vocational training programs: hotel—motel management, greenhouse and nursery work, arts and crafts, auto mechanics, home health aides, and building maintenance. Another 35 people went into work experience situations with government or nonprofit agencies. They were clerk typists, groundskeepers, and receptionists for city or county government, the forestry service, or agencies like the American Cancer Society or the Red Cross. Forty-three took OJT slots as janitors or maintenance workers in nursing homes or senior citizen villages, or did clerical or sales work with retail stores or private businesses. There were 13 reentries, clients from the previous year who were returning for additional training.

During the course of the year 48 clients dropped out: 2 left to go to school, 1 dropped out because of poor attendance, and the rest left because of their own illness or illness in the family which required their attention. The remaining 141 got jobs, for a placement rate of 75 percent. Retention rates were 95 percent at 60 days and 88 percent after 120 days.

The two most successful training programs are for home health aides and building maintenance workers. The thrust of the former is to provide home health aides for incapacitated senior citizens and thus reduce the likelihood of institutionalization. Handicapped and blind individuals are also served. The eight-week class is run by two registered nurses who teach cardio-pulmonary resuscitation, care of diabetics, and simple nursing skills—bed baths, feeding, light exercise, and the transfer of nonambulatory patients. Cleaning and light housekeeping tasks are also included. Both men and women attend this class, and most get jobs with private families.

The building maintenance class meets for 12 weeks. Vocational trainers teach general janitorial and repair skills—some plumbing, carpentry, and painting. Graduates of this program can fix broken doors and windows, repair leaky sinks and broken locks, and take care of exterior and interior painting. They work in private and convalescent homes, or at UPKEEP, a retirement community for people over 60 with limited incomes.

In 1978 OAETC's program was restructured. While the home health aide and building maintenance classes are still on-site programs, all other training is by referral to other agencies. The two on-site classes have been opened to all age groups and now serve adults over 18. Placement is handled by FETC via a central order-taking system run by the California Employment Development Department. According to Kenneth Woods at FETC, placement rates for senior citizens are much lower than for other population groups because the agency's object is to find permanent, full-time jobs for its clients, whereas many older workers prefer only part-time jobs to "supplement their Social Security income." Thus no senior citizens are getting OJT or work experience slots. Overall placement, including that of older workers, is "about 60 to 65 percent," says Woods. Figures for older workers alone have not been broken out of the total number. Older graduates of the home health aide program, he reports, are more apt to take jobs with private families, while the younger ones go into hospitals and convalescent homes, which they believe will lead to a career.

Dee Lockhardt, Director of OAETC, deplores the fragmentation of services. She believes that the job developer should be in contact with the client throughout the training period. She is concerned that the shift in CETA funding toward youth, and the lack of eligibility of many senior citizens for CETA training because of their Social Security income, will make job placement increasingly difficult. "I am afraid that older workers are getting lost in the shuffle," she says.

SENIOR PERSONNEL EMPLOYMENT COUNCIL OF WESTCHESTER

An Old Idea Finds New Followers

This nonprofit employment service was founded in 1955 by Selene Rosenberg, a Scarsdale resident with a marketing background who thought unemployed senior citizens represented the waste of a potential and important resource. With the help of the White Plains Council of Community Services, Senior Personnel Employment Council of West-chester (SPEC) was incorporated and has functioned ever since as a free community service under the direction of a volunteer board of directors. John J. Blanchfield, SPEC's executive director, says he believes it is the oldest agency of its kind in the country and that it has served as the model for at least 100 others. In April 1979 the National Association of Older Worker Employment Services was formed under the aegis of the National Council on Aging, with Blanchfield as president. One of the new organization's priorities is a legislative proposal to change the CETA regulations which consider Social Security as income and thus eliminate many older workers from CETA programs.

SPEC operates a regional office in the county seat of White Plains with five affiliates in surrounding towns. Senior Personnel has interviewed over 10,000 senior citizens in the last 25 years, and has placed 7000 of them in part-time, or temporary jobs. It is estimated that over $15 million has been returned to the local economy as a result of salaries earned by Senior Personnel placements, substantial evidence that the Council's motto, "Ability is Ageless," is valid.

The regional office staff includes the executive director, a secretary, 14 volunteer job counselors, and one volunteer controller. Until recently, SPEC was virtually unable to place its clients with any of the large corporations headquartered in Westchester because most had mandatory retirement policies which prohibited hiring older workers. Blanchfield says this is changing. In 1979 SPEC placed two secretaries and four clerical workers with two major corporations for periods of between four and six months. Blanchfield believes this is because of a shortage of entry-level workers, who tend to leave the county because of extraordinarily high housing costs. The statistics bear him out. Twenty percent of Westchester's 890,000 inhabitants are over the age of 60.

In the past SPEC has found jobs for its clients with small- and medium-sized businesses and retail stores. The job categories have been varied, including typists, bookkeepers, accountants, drafters, engineers, secretaries, sales personnel, stock clerks, cashiers, maintenance workers, and gardeners. Two special services—paid neighbors and paid grandmothers—provide companions for the elderly and recuperating individuals and baby sitters, respectively.

The volunteer job counselors, all senior citizens themselves, are trained in interviewing techniques. There are no forms for clients to fill out; each person has an informal 20-minute chat with a job counselor, who notes the client's skills and determines job preferences, locations, and when the person is available for work. This information is transferred to a file card, which becomes the permanent record. Almost all SPEC jobs are temporary and part time due to two limiting factors—ERISA requirements, which mandate that a company extend fringe benefits to any employee who works more than 1000 hours per year, and Social Security rules, which penalized anyone who earned more than $375 per month in 1979.

Clients find out about Senior Personnel through posters, brochures, flyers in banks, stores, public buildings and churches, articles in the local press, radio, TV community service announcements, and inserts which accompany monthly utility bills. Most people work because they must. A 1975 survey of 200 SPEC applicants found that 80 percent needed the money. Some are bitter about this, or ashamed, and ask for jobs out of their own neighborhoods. Inflation is aggravating the situation. The number of applicants at the regional office rose to 1200 last year, a 33 percent jump from the year before.

Senior Personnel has various sources of funds, which include the United Way of Westchester, the Westchester Office of Manpower Development, private foundations and contributions from "Friends of Senior Personnel."

RETIREMENT JOBS, INC.

In 1979, approximately 15,000 jobs in the San Francisco Bay Area were filled by older people, especially retirees, through the referral services of Retirement Jobs, Inc.* When this nonprofit organization was founded in 1962, it had a single suburban office. Today, it has 18 offices located throughout the five Bay Area counties.

"It is very difficult for older people to find jobs," says Harold Adams, vice-president and executive director of Retirement Jobs. "Social Security payments are not enough to keep pace with today's continuing inflation, and many senior citizens feel the need to supplement that income through part-time work. However, there is growing awareness that retirees form the largest pool of untapped experience in the country, and both business leaders and private citizens are now accepting this fact."

*Reprinted from *Training and Jobs Programs in Action* by David Robison (New York: Committee for Economic Development in cooperation with Work in America Institute, Inc., 1978).

The agency's services have grown steadily both in numbers of people served and in the range of programs offered. The largest increase has occurred since 1975. Retirement Jobs filled about 6000 jobs that year. In 1977, it doubled its output to about 12,000 placements, with a monthly average of 1000 referrals. The branch offices play the major role in job search and recruitment and in placing applicants in jobs that are consistent with their past work experience. As a staff member remarked, "The state employment offices often send their older job applicants to us because they, too, find it very difficult to place people age 55 and older, or even people over age 50."

With the aid of federal departments that administer CETA projects, Retirement Jobs has been able to hire a number of men and women to serve as outreach workers. They canvass the communities to develop job opportunities for people 55 and over. In addition, a quarterly newsletter is distributed to public and private agencies, citizens organizations, libraries, legislators, and municipal officials.

Retirement Jobs is supported by donations and grants from cities, private foundations, individuals, clients, and older workers who have found jobs through the organization. "When people get to know about what we are trying to do," Adams says, "they invariably want to contribute. In the larger cities such as San Francisco and Oakland, the business communities have been of tremendous financial assistance; in the suburban areas, individuals have responded in a most generous manner." For example, the Lockheed Corporation has donated an office in its complex in Sunnyvale, California which is used by many Lockheed retirees and other local residents.

Retirement Jobs has other activities besides referrals. Under Title XX of the 1974 Social Services Amendments, it holds contracts with two counties to recruit, schedule, and match workers, especially older workers, to the homemaking needs of older and handicapped citizens; about 300 workers are providing homemaking assistance under this program. Another 400 are performing similar services in Contra Costa County under an agreement administered by the Council on Aging in that area. These programs meet the needs of many older people by providing services that make it possible for them to remain in their homes and in a familiar environment and to retain the dignity so essential to their continued welfare. Such a solution is far better for these older people than institutionalization, and is considerably less expensive for the community.

Retirement Jobs has also developed several programs that were begun by senior citizens organizations, civic groups, and other interested groups. One of these is the Senior Home Repair Service, which is administered by the Senior Coordinating Council of Palo Alto. Through the council, Palo Alto citizens who are 60 years old or older can have minor home repairs made at very reasonable prices. The rates vary according to the homeowner's income, and for those whose incomes are minimal, the city of Palo Alto subsidizes whatever costs are necessary for the required work.

4
Redeployment

Rapidly altering social and economic conditions are producing movement both within and between business organizations at a greater pace than ever before. This section deals with two aspects of that movement, both of them involuntary. The first, outplacement, is the direct effort of management to provide counseling and relocation assistance to surplus employees. The second, reassignment to positions of lesser responsibility, or demotion, is a still-tenuous personnel response which attempts to harmonize the changing needs of the organization and its work force while avoiding termination. In the majority of cases described here, the cause of the dislocation had to do with economic imperatives and was outside the individual worker's competence—for instance, termination may have resulted from a closed plant, a terminated research and development program, or a recession-inspired personnel cutback.

It is interesting to note that while termination and demotion represent some of the harshest medicine in the corporate experience, the results can be positive. A study by Fuchs, Cuthrel and Company of 250 outplaced clients found that 88 percent of them got jobs with higher pay than their exit salaries; and a study by Dr. Donald Monaco of Drake-Beam and Associates, using a smaller sample bears him out. Results like these, as well as humane considerations, make a strong case for outplacement counseling assistance to ease the trauma of separation. However, these cheerful statistics do not necessarily bode well for the older, outplaced employee, whose time between jobs is demonstrably longer than that of younger colleagues, and who generally has a harder time accepting the reality of the job loss, as evidenced by the disorientation of long-service employees faced with the plant closing described in this unit.

Age seems also to play a part in the acceptance of demotion as an alternative to early retirement or termination. In Denmark, for instance, the older the worker, the more likely he or she is to agree to a reassignment that involves less responsibility and pay. The point that a flexible rather than a fixed retirement age would make it easier for individuals to indulge in periods of upward and downward mobility at different career stages is well taken and should be considered by American managers.

Finally, it is important to underline that, where demotion has worked successfully in this country, there have been three principles at work; mutual consent, time for exploration of alternatives and options, and the ability to transfer to another unit within the company to avoid peer pressure and publicity.

Outplacement

Professional Help which Benefits Companies and Employees

The term outplacement and the idea behind it first surfaced in the late 1960s when simultaneous cuts in space exploration and defense spending led to wholesale job terminations of engineers and technical employees in the aerospace and related industries. Since then a number of business conditions have combined to make this new personnel service a growth industry of its own. They include the 1974-75 recession which triggered significant personnel cutbacks; numerous mergers and acquisitions and the consequent duplication of executive positions; a slower growth in the economy which calls for cost-effective corporate planning, leaner staffing, and greater accountability on the part of management. Added to these are the garden-variety reasons for job termination—plant closings, policy disputes, and personality clashes. In this climate it is usually not incompetence which leads to personnel displacement but changing business conditions. Whatever the reasons, it is the older employee who is most often adversely affected.

Outplacement is the extension to terminated employees of professional counseling services to minimize the emotional shock and impact of the job loss, reduce the amount of time needed to find a new position, improve the individual's job-search skills, and bring about the best possible match between the person and available jobs. Individual counseling is provided for executives earning $30,000 and more a year, while a group approach is used when the dislocation involves substantial numbers of employees.

Authorities in the human resources field differ about the best way to implement outplacement services. Carl Driessnack, Managing Consultant of THinc Career Planning Corporation, gives several reasons for the use of qualified outside consultants. The outplacement process is time consuming, he says, while the company's need is intermittent, making it difficult for an in-house personnel department to accumulate the requisite expertise and versatility to do the job right. He sees an advantage in having the terminated individual conduct the job search away from the company's premises, both in terms of personal sensitivities and the effect on ex-colleagues. John Sherba, vice-president of the First National Bank of Akron, disagrees, pointing out that the in-house approach has several advantages. It reduces the antagonism of the departed employee, improves the company's image with its remaining staff, its customers and the community, and decreases unemployment compensation costs. David Switkin, director of outplacement counseling at Citibank, adds that the in-house method is cost effective, running at about 4 percent of the terminated employee's salary as compared to the 10 to 12 percent charged by consulting firms.

Whatever the method, the use and acceptability of outplacement is growing. According to Dr. Donald Monaco, senior vice-president of Drake-Beam and Associates and director of its outplacement services, the number of clients referred to his firm by Fortune 500 companies is doubling annually. Hundreds of businesses are using outplacement, from major oil companies to insurance firms, utilities, banks, hospitals, the New York Stock Exchange, the United Presbyterian Church, universities, and government agencies, including the United States Department of State. And more people are beginning to see the positive aspects of this service. James Gallagher of Career Management Associates sums it up as follows: "Being fired is not the death of a career; I'd say it's often the factor that gives a career new life." And Monaco adds, "There are times when it is good for an individual to separate from the corporation. When a person has plateaued, staying on is often wasteful."

Outplacement Counseling Firms: Methods and Findings

A survey of four leading outplacement firms—THinc Career Planning Corporation, Fuchs, Cuthrell and Company, Inc., Drake-Beam and Associates, and Career Management Associates—indicates more similarities than differences in technique.

There are two main stages in outplacement counseling. The first is the predetermination interview. The purpose here is threefold: to get to know the prospective client through interviews with superiors and employee records, to assist the supervisor in planning the termination interview, and to be waiting in the wings with immediate help for the employee. Reactions include shock, anger, fear, and a terrible sense of loss—of identity, empire, and face.

To combat these negative feelings, outplacement counselors move their clients immediately into the second phase—mobilization. This starts with daily counseling sessions during which past accomplishments are put on paper to remind clients of their strengths and abilities. This skills assessment is augmented by in-depth interviews, testing, and identification of developmental needs and goals. Résumés are written and markets are investigated. Outplacement counselors find personal contacts in the form of letters and phone calls the best source of information about jobs. All agree that 80 to 90 percent of existing employment opportunities are never publicized and urge their clients to contact friends, schoolmates, relatives, former associates, and members of professional organizations and clubs. Jim Fuchs recommends the indirect approach. "You work under the assumption that you're not seeing this person to ask for a job. You're going to introduce yourself and ask for advice." Fuchs recommends careful preparation for the interview—background reading about the industry involved, job skills required, and available opportunities, as well as personal information about the individual being seen. Monaco uses audiovisual interview training and then urges clients to get on the phone to make appointments. And Gallagher reminds his clients that "we use our friendships all the time to get things we want. Why should this be different?"

Results

The counseling process continues until placement. Two outplacement counselors who reviewed their caseloads came up with the following statistical information. Fuchs' study of 250 clients who got jobs found that 88 percent were making more than their exit salaries, 12 percent were getting the same pay, and two-thirds of those placements were in jobs that had not existed before. He credits the indirect interview approach for this latter statistic, saying that clients who make a strong impression frequently convince the interviewer that they are "too good to lose."

Monaco's more detailed information is based on a sample of 200 clients referred to his company by large corporations. Within four to six months, two-thirds (132 people) found new jobs. Salary comparisons show that 71 percent of those individuals were earning more than they had been, 21 people were receiving the same pay, 10 were making less, and 15 had decided on a career change which involved going into business for themselves. The average age of this group was 45, the average salary, $51,000.

Monaco says that only 2 to 5 percent of his clients are over 55, and he admits that older executives have a harder time finding jobs. He points out that the older executive is at a higher level of experience and pay, where there are fewer openings. To help individuals through this difficult time, Drake-Beam advises putting severance pay on a monthly basis so that income continues during the search period.

Client satisfaction with outplacement counseling firms is substantiated by growing referrals. One large manufacturer of consumer products, with 20,000 employees and annual sales of $1.5 billion reports that in the last three years it has terminated 60 people, a handful of executives each year plus an entire research and development department. With the help of outside outplacement counseling these employees, whose exit salaries averaged $30,000, received compensation that was 5 percent higher in their new jobs.

In-House Outplacement Services

When a diversified corporation which manufactures products for the housing, construction, and automotive industries closed an antiquated plant in July 1978, the personnel department was charged with providing outplacement services to 65 salaried employees caught by the reduction in force. This company is a large one, with sales of just under $5 billion, an international work force of 113,000, and 55,000 domestic employees. The plant in question had 1100 workers, of whom 245 were salaried and 855 were represented employees.

The breakdown for the salaried staff was as follows: 100 were able to transfer into other divisions within the company, 25 retired, and 55 went back into the bargaining unit. The personnel department had three months to work with the remaining 65 employees.

Before beginning outplacement counseling sessions, each terminated worker met with personnel representatives, who explained the worker's rights regarding severance pay, pension eligibility, pension contribution funds, and life and medical insurance. A complete manual was developed which covered job-search techniques: how and where to gather information about employment opportunities; how to write résumés and letters of inquiry, with samples; how to fill out application forms correctly and completely; self-appraisal exercises, which included tips on goal setting, decision making, time management, and values clarification; and how to handle appointments and job interviews. Counseling sessions went into these areas in greater depth.

Individual needs varied widely. Some people were able to organize and manage an effective job-search campaign without the counseling sessions, using only the manual; some attended only a few sessions; and one man had five individual appointments during which he wrote his résumé, made calls, filled out job applications, practiced interviewing, and wrote follow-up letters, culminating in several job offers. Most of the clients averaged only one or two group meetings and used the outplacement service only until their résumés were developed and typed.

The personnel staff found that while the younger workers were able to handle the situation, older, long-service employees experienced considerable trauma. Some needed help in understanding that the plant was really closing and that, although the company would help them, finding another job was up to them. These individuals, though they clearly needed the most help, did not seek it.

Although there was no formal follow-up after the plant closed, 23 of the group receiving outplacement help reported that they found other jobs. According to the program director, they included maintenance workers, skilled trade supervisors, engineers, and clerical staff. Supervisors and production workers had the most difficulty finding new jobs. While a few of the 23 successful job searchers were over 40, most were younger. The program director felt that the plant closing was infinitely harder on the older employees.

Union representatives reported the same results. The president of the local bargaining unit said that 400 of the represented employees were absorbed by another plant in the same city and 50 were eligible for preferential hiring at other manufacturing facilities around the country represented by the union. Younger workers without families took advantage of this opportunity while older workers who tried to do the same had severe personal problems. There were several threatened divorces over moving. More than 400 people in the area are still on recall. They have taken jobs with smaller companies but are hoping things will pick up in the future.

Reassignment To Positions Of Lesser Responsibility (Demotion)

The concept of demotion sounds mildly subversive. Because Americans tend to equate success in life with a better job, a more elegant title, and a bigger salary, the very idea of demotion seems to go against the country's basic value structure. Although no one debates the fact that real life proceeds on an inevitable bell-shaped curve, an exemplary work life is presumed to have only one direction—up.

However, scarcity, unemployment, declining productivity, a slower rate of economic growth, and the idea that sources of personal satisfaction exist beyond the workplace, are combining to allow limited experimentation with demotion by agreement, or, as it is sometimes called, downplacement or deescalation.

THE DANISH EXPERIENCE

This singular view of mobility is not solely an American dilemma. Similar concerns in Europe prompted the Danish Institute for Personnel Management (DIPM) to conduct a study in 1978 aimed at exploring how managers themselves felt about demotion.* They surveyed 1285 execu-

* Laurids Hedaa. "Danish Survey Suggests Demotion for 'Obsolete' Managers; Finds Execs Prefer Lesser Jobs to Retirement." *World of Work Report* 3 (November 1978).

tives at 154 of Denmark's largest companies. When these individuals were asked whether they preferred demotion to early retirement, a resounding 70 percent said yes.

Laurids Hedaa, executive vice-president of DIPM and both a research officer and member of the executive committee of the European Association for Personnel Management, has observed that there are limited options for dealing with obsolete executives: accept the situation; retrain, move, fire, or retire the manager; or redesign the job. Competitive business conditions make the first two alternatives unlikely, says Hedaa, and job redesign at the executive level means limiting work and responsibility within the confines of the same position, a difficult if not impossible goal to achieve. Firing the manager is inhumane and has deleterious effects on other employees, and early retirement is so expensive that it remains an option of only the largest and most prosperous companies. That, reasons Hedaa, leaves transfer which, for the aging executive, inevitably involves demotion.

The Danish survey population was 95 percent male; 35 percent were under 40, 38 percent were between the ages of 40 and 54, and 26 percent were over 55. They ranged from top-level to line managers in companies with work forces which averaged 1300 employees. All branches of industry were represented.

The central question asked was "What would your reactions be if you were told that you would now be transferred to a different job, which it might be assumed would demand less competence and would be of a lower status than your present job?"

Those surveyed were asked to respond to the questions asked with one of the following reactions:
1. Accept without question.
2. Reduce the work effort.
3. Work harder to be promoted again.
4. Seek other employment.

Reactions Vary with Age

When the prospect of being replaced by a younger executive did not include a change in job title or a reduction in salary, nearly three-quarters of the executives over the age of 54 indicated that they would accept the change in jobs (reaction 1), compared with 46 percent of those between the ages of 40 and 54, and only 18 percent of the executives under the age of 40.

When these executives were also informed that they would be downgraded in title and responsibility and their salaries reduced by 10 percent, their reactions were as follows:

Reaction Pattern (%)

Group	1	2	3	4
Under 40 years	4	3	8	83
40–54 years	14	18	14	50
55 and over	28	28	13	18
Top managers	14	12	11	53
Middle managers	13	16	11	55
Line managers	16	17	13	50
Average	14	15	11	54

Twenty-eight percent of the managers over 55 years old would accept demotion without any further question (reaction 1), and the same proportion would accept it with reduced work effort (reaction 2). Thirteen percent would work hard to establish the former working conditions (reaction 3), and 18 percent would look for another job (reaction 4).

It is quite clear from this chart that the downgrading, presented to a manager without any sugarcoating, is accepted to a higher degree the older the manager is.

Thirty-one percent of the managers over 55 saw no advantage to demotion. Some 28 percent, however, observed that there would be less strain on health; 21 percent foresaw that physical and mental burdens would be reduced; and 15 percent believed that there would be more opportunity to deal with non-job-related interests.

The disadvantages managers over 55 saw as resulting from demotion were: less challenge (29 percent); loss of self-respect (27 percent); and reduced income (24 percent).

Nevertheless, when offered one of only two choices, working in a downgraded position with a 10 percent reduction in salary or early retirement with a 40 percent reduction in salary (the difference in salaries is minor due to Danish tax laws), as many as 70 percent of the managers over 55 opted for the downgraded position. Eternal leisure is, apparently, only attractive at a comfortable distance.

One way of reconciling the needs of the corporation with the needs of the aging manager is the abolition of the fixed pensionable age. This adjustment in the pension system could make it possible for obsolete managers to be pensioned earlier, thus making it possible for them to accept loss of status without an accompanying loss of self-respect.

The problem is that many of the personnel policies commonplace in the business world today are based on the assumption that working capacity increases with age until retirement, at which time it declines (literally overnight) to such a degree that the manager is of no further use to the organization. Despite the absurdity of this model, age continues to be the sole criterion for retirement in almost all occupations.

A much more workable model is one in which job requirements are graphed against the pensionable age. A simplified version of this model appears below.

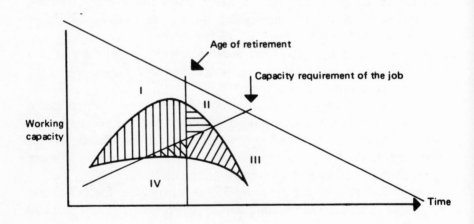

Four theoretical groups of workers are represented. Group I includes those whose working capacity exceeds the job requirements, and who are all under the retirement age. Group II is composed of highly productive workers who have passed the retirement age. Similarly, groups III and IV represent workers who produce less than is required of them and who are, respectively, above and below the retirement age.

If a flexible pensionable age were adopted, pensions would be granted when the working capacity of a given worker was permanently situated below the job requirements—in the groups identified as III and IV. In turn, this would alter the circumstances under which transfer to a less demanding job is considered a viable alternative, because both the upper and lower age limits for retirement could be extended.

In support of this concept, 63 percent of the executives questioned in the survey described earlier felt that society at large should decide on a flexible pensionable age. Only 1 out of every 20 executives felt that Denmark's present policy of retirement at 67 was the correct age, with 31 percent indicating a preference for a younger age.

In depth research as well as debate will be necessary before companies can establish more flexible career patterns that allow downward mobility to be as natural as upward mobility. Inevitably, this research will also lead to consideration of changes in the pension system. Hopefully, the study undertaken by the Danish Institute for Personnel Management has broken the ground for serious consideration of new policies that will permit companies to make full use of their entire leadership potential in an increasingly competitive business climate.

MAREMONT CORPORATION

A Pragmatic Policy

Maremont manufactures ordinance parts for machine guns and automotive components at its three production facilities in Oklahoma, Tennessee, and Maine. Headquartered in Chicago, the company employs 7500 people, 2000 of whom are salaried staff. Annual sales are $375 million.

Ten years ago Maremont stumbled upon demotion by agreement, which it prefers to call downplacement. An outstanding salesman who had been a star performer for years was rewarded with a slot as manager. Since he lacked leadership skills and had trouble delegating authority, the promotion proved to be disastrous. Management offered him a choice between outplacement and going back to his old job. He was 40 years old at the time and elected to stay with the company at a salary which was reduced by $1000 a year. To avoid the inevitable peer pressure, he moved to a different division in another location, where he again became a super salesman, winning one of the company's prized awards within a couple of years. He is still a valued employee.

Maremont management was so impressed with this success story that, over the last ten years, it has offered the same choice to about 25 people who have accepted downplacement in preference to termination. All were in their forties or fifties. For about half the people, downgrading did not work and the employees subsequently left the company. According to T. C. Sullivan, vice-president of personnel and industrial relations, these were all situations in which the demoted individuals were highly visible in managerial roles and stayed in the same unit. One case involved a plant manager who became a departmental manager; another was a sales manager who reverted to salesman. There was an accounts supervisor who returned to the position of accountant and an operations supervisor who went into data processing. In all cases, Sullivan says, the involved employees could not accept what they perceived as public humiliation.

However, the downplacement process has worked well where the affected employee was given a choice, could move to another location, and received counseling during the adjustment process. In dealing with these employees Sullivan stresses the matter of choice, pointing out that the person can stay with the company in another capacity, or leave, and that the company will help with either decision. The only thing the individual cannot do is remain in the same job. His observation is that managers experience the greatest difficulty not with the actual jobs involved but with the values of promotion and success that are so deeply ingrained in our society. Until these start to change, he feels, demotion will be a tool with only marginal acceptance.

THE KELLOGG COMPANY

Consultation and Choice Help Employees Accept Demotion

Known primarily for its cereals, Kellogg is actually a diversified manu-facturer of convenience foods, among them institutional food products, soup bases, and frozen foods. The company grosses $1.75 billion annually and employs over 7000 people in the United States, most of them in Battle Creek, Michigan, where Kellogg is the major employer.

Demotion is an unusual practice, but can occur if an employee elects to apply for, and is selected to fill, a vacancy within the company at a lower level than the present job. A company-sponsored program permits inter-nal advertising of vacancies before applicants from outside the organiza-tion are sought. When a demotion occurs as a result of an employee's voluntarily applying for an internal job, the employee's salary is adjusted immediately to the rate applicable to the new job.

Demotion also takes place in two other ways: (1) if significant reor-ganization or technological changes make it impossible to continue employees in present jobs, they may be shifted to jobs at lower levels, to the mutual benefit of both employee and company; and (2) if an employee simply cannot handle increased responsibilities, but has a track record indicating a commendable performance at a lower level of job responsi-bility, he or she may be demoted to a job at that level. In both of these examples of demotion, the prior job performance of the individuals, as well as the particular circumstances of each situation, are essential factors in deciding whether to demote or terminate.

Except when demotion occurs entirely voluntarily, each individual is consulted in an attempt to provide as wide a range of options as possible, for example, demotion vs. relocation, termination, etc. At the same time, continuation of the higher salary normally is extended for periods of up to one year to permit time for the employee to adjust.

Dave Walbridge, manager of organization planning at Kellogg, be-lieves that the company's role as the foremost employer in Battle Creek is a major factor in making demotion an attractive alternative for employees. The company also benefits from "demotion by agreement" because it can utilize the experience of long-time employees and thus minimize recruiting and training expenses.

A total of approximately 12 people were placed during 1979 in accordance with the demotion arrangements.

GENERAL ELECTRIC COMPANY—AIRCRAFT ENGINE GROUP

Recession and Demotion

A limited experience with demotion occurred at GE's Aircraft Engine Group during the 1971–72 economic slowdown. This operation then employed 28,000 people at major locations in Massachusetts and Ohio, and at satellite operations in six other states. About 9000 individuals, comprising the exempt salaried group and including managers, engineers, supervisors, and functional specialists, were hardest hit by the 20 percent reduction in work force that faced the entire operation.

If a separated employee is forced to accept a job in another company that is poorly compensated in comparison to the employee's GE job, it is company policy to supplement the new salary for a period of time as a "salary bridge." R. W. Haskell, manager of organization development, says the firm had only modest success in convincing managerial employees that, in the long run, the temporary benefits of the salary bridge were not as advantageous as accepting demotion, staying with the company, and waiting for economic conditions to improve. Only a few hundred employees opted for lesser jobs at GE, stepping back into the ranks of the hourly and nonexempt workers. Typically, supervisors, managers, and superintendents became machinists, clerks, and drafters.

The trauma was most apparent when the decision became public. Haskell says it is peer reaction that makes demotion so painful, even when it occurs because of economic conditions and involves a large group of people. Subsequently, all of the demoted employees returned to exempt slots as the economy improved and opportunities for promotion became available.

5
The New "New-Hires"— Older Workers

Demographers are warning the nation that by the end of the century there will be a significant shortage of younger workers and a concomitant demand for experienced personnel. There are signs that the country is shifting away from its well-advertised "youth culture" to one that will make age and wisdom respectable again. Terms like the "graying of America" and the "aging eighties" are becoming clichés. New magazines called *Fifty Plus*, *Prime Time*, *Modern Maturity*, and *Dynamic Years* sit next to *Redbook* and *McCalls* on the newsstand. Organizations abound—the National Council on the Aging, the Center for Work and Aging, the National Committee on Careers for Older Americans, the American Association of Retired Persons, to name a few. A prime-time television show, "Over Easy," explores social issues and problems faced by senior citizens and celebrates the lives of productive older Americans. TV commercials feature older people in ads that push everything from arthritis remedies to pantyhose. The flood of women entering the labor force is in large part a movement of older workers. The ADEA amendment itself gives individuals rather than employers the right to decide how long they will work.

Some industries are hiring older workers and annuitants right now. Where skills are in short supply, in engineering and high technology fields, secretarial and clerical work, and skilled craft areas, age does not appear to be a significant factor. As long as people are physically able to do their jobs, employers do not seem to care how old they are. Some personnel directors even seek older "new-hires." Daniel Knowles, director of personnel at Grumman Aircraft Corporation says, "There has to be a correlation between age, experience, and performance. A 40-year-old worker is mature and realistic, knows limitations and will stick to a task. You need three career-development analysts to steady a youngster just out of school." And in company after company, personnel directors are reporting high manager satisfaction with older worker productivity and reliability. What John D. MacArthur, chairman of the board of Bankers Life and Casualty Company, told a presidential committee in 1954 was underscored by Gerald Maguire, the company's vice-president of corporate services at a 1977 House subcommittee hearing on aging: "Older workers are more dependable, have better attendance records, stay on the job longer, and do as much work as the younger element."

There are two kinds of employment which older workers and annuitants seek today. One is full time and includes many different types of people and jobs—individuals who change companies and careers after 40, women who have raised families, and early retirees who go right back to work. The other is part time and its purpose is to supplement retirement income and relieve boredom.

High Technology Industries

SUNDSTRAND DATA CONTROL, INC.

This aerospace electronics firm makes avionic computer systems, airborne recorders and flight data systems for commercial and military aircraft, flight recorders, and a variety of measurement devices (accelerometers, transducers, thermal switches) for use in aerospace, ground transportation, and the petrochemical industry. Located in the state of Washington, Sundstrand employs 1600 people and is experiencing shortages of electronic and mechanical design engineers, drafters, circuit board designers and assemblers, skilled electronic technicians, and precision mechanical assemblers.

To combat this situation Gary Hedges, Sundstrand's personnel manager, began recruiting older workers and retirees in three ways: among the company's own annuitants, through a contract engineering employment firm in Seattle, and via newspaper ads which read, "Retired? Sundstrand needs you."

The greatest number of recruits have come through the contract engineering firm. Over the past three years, Sundstrand has had between 30 and 40 employees on contract in the above-named categories. When the company finds someone it wants to hire as a permanent employee, it is free to do so after 90 days without further fees to the contracting company. Hedges has hired two 67-year-old engineers in this manner.

Because Sundstrand has a young work force it has only 35 annuitants. Six of these have come back to work, three engineers, one supervisor, one assembler, and one 69-year-old machinist. These workers have a choice regarding compensation. They can be considered temporary employees, receive an hourly wage and continue to draw their pensions. Or they can return as full-time workers, receive their salaries and fringe benefits, stop the pension while continuing to accrue credits toward a second retirement.

The newspaper ads have not been effective as yet, but Hedges is hoping to get some response. At the moment, he has between 20 and 40 jobs waiting to be filled.

AEROSPACE CORPORATION

Aerospace hires annuitants as short-term consultants under a general policy which limits them to 20 working days a year. The company is looking for about 400 engineers and scientists in a broad range of specialties. Of the 100 consultants on staff in 1979, between 30 and 50 were Aerospace annuitants, a few were retirees from other companies. Not all of these people are used in technical capacities. Robert Rubenstein, who runs Aerospace's preretirement program, employs four each year as speakers in the retirement-planning workshop.

Special contracts are written for annuitants who work for longer time periods. Last year the corporation's former controller returned to head the materials department, which handles purchasing and contracting, while the regular manager of that department was recovering from a heart attack. His contract ran for four months. In mid-1979 Aerospace hired a 67-year-old annuitant who is an optics expert. This man, who had retired reluctantly at age 65 under previous company policy, had been serving as a short-term consultant for the intervening two years. As a regular employee he receives salary and fringe benefits; his pension, which is a defined benefit plan, ceases and no new credits accumulate during this second period of employment.

According to Rubenstein, annuitants come back to Aerospace for a number of reasons—boredom, money, challenge. Some find their retirement incomes inadequate in the face of inflation, and others find retirement a disappointment. One annuitant, who took early retirement to build his own sailboat and sail around the world, returned two years later to ask for (and get) his old job back. He missed the challenge of work.

LOCKHEED CORPORATION

This giant aircraft company employs 60,000 people, 26,000 in the exempt category and 34,000 nonexempt workers. There are eight operating divisions in California, Washington State, Georgia, New Jersey, and Texas. The company has a stable work force, 57 percent of whom are over the age of 45. Like all aerospace companies, Lockheed suffers from a shortage of engineers and skilled craft workers. Howard Lockwood, corporate director of management development, says that age is not a factor in hiring. His analysis of 1979 new-hires at a major California location shows that 293 were over the age of 50. This number included 12 retirees and some rehires. They were hired into a wide variety of jobs, as the following table illustrates.

Age	Sex	Job Description
57	M	Supervisor of manufacturing
61	M	Design division engineer
58	F	Structures installation—trainee
59	M	Methods and time standards engineer
57	F	General clerk typist
60	M	Design specialist
55	M	Structures and instruments worker—trainee
57	M	Planner of structures and fabrication
54	F	Plastics helper
62	M	Mock-up tooling development mechanic
51	M	Electronic systems technician—flight
54	F	Custodian—light

NORTHROP CORPORATION

Northrop manufactures aircraft, electronics equipment, computers, and support services to go with them. With annual sales in the 1.6 billion range, Northrop employs 35,000 workers in 15 domestic locations. The overseas force is about 2000.

The company maintains an on-call work force of retired and former company employees which provides personnel for areas of high need in limited time frames. This is used in conjunction with a skills roster of retirees. Individuals on the on-call work force may work up to 60 days, after which they must take 30 days off. Employees work a full shift, eight hours during the day, six at night. About 300 people in the company's southern California location make up this force, which includes workers who have gone back to school as well as annuitants. They take jobs as machinists, work in sheet-metal fabrication, and occupy temporary clerical positions. Those who have retired receive an hourly wage and keep their pension; they can also rejoin the company's savings plan.

GENERAL ELECTRIC COMPANY—AIRCRAFT ENGINE GROUP

This operating group of GE, with a work force of 28,000 people, maintains a fluctuating retainer capability currently ranging from 25 to 30 annuitants who have technical and managerial skills the company does not want to lose. Individuals are paid a yearly retainer based on between 20 and 100 days per year at a daily rate that is pegged to their salary at the time of retirement. Examples of annuitants using this arrangement include a former field sales manager who had built up a particularly good relationship with a major commercial customer, a former general manager who has just completed a salary reconciliation which compared cross-functions and appropriate salary relationships of the top 5 percent of the exempt group, a shaft balancer, and a former manager of contracts who trains marketing and contracts personnel in negotiating skills.

SUN COMPANY

When Robert N. Custer, director of retiree relations, announced in the retiree newsletter in early 1979 that the company would be hiring annuitants for temporary jobs, he expected a meager response. Instead,

600 people contacted his office. This represented almost 10 percent of the company's annuitants. Sun, the nation's tenth largest oil company, employs 35,000 people.

In the last two years 200 people have found temporary jobs, and about 100 are on the payroll at any given time. The positions have been at all levels, from an executive who is working four half-days a week managing a warehousing facility, to engineers and scientists working on special projects. Many clerical and secretarial workers have been placed, as well as a few production people. Individual contracts are written for each temporary employee, most of whom are paid an hourly wage.

Custer reports that his field managers are pleased with these employees. "They've done their jobs better than the hiring managers expected. Some were afraid of having little old ladies or men tottering around. But these people came in full of vigor, gave a full eight hours of work with no two-hour coffee breaks and long lunches. They were happy to be working again and wanted to do well so that they'd be called back."

Custer's biggest problem now is creating a data bank of retiree skills so that they can be matched via computer with the hundreds of temporary jobs that come up each year. With his small office staff he is not sure how long that will take. But he is certain it is the wave of the future. "There's a vast storehouse of skills and knowledge in the retired people of this country," says Custer. "The trick is to get at it."

PENNSYLVANIA POWER AND LIGHT COMPANY

This private, stockholder-owned utility operates six power plants and five division service centers in the eastern part of the state. The general office complex is in Allentown, where one-fourth of the 7500 employees of the company are located. Pennsylvania Power and Light has grown rapidly in the last ten years, adding 2500 new employees, most of them entry-level workers. The average age of the work force is 30.

However, Donald L. Walker, employee relations manager, reports a new development in hiring during the last year. Of the 50 engineers taken on in 1978–79, 10 were over 40. All had skills in the various engineering disciplines—mechanical, electrical, civil, nuclear—and had been working for consulting firms. Walker believes that tighter budgets and a consequent drop in consulting contracts combined with what he calls "the natural desire of men around 40 for stability," caused these workers to seek permanent employment. Supply side-factors meshed with changes in company attitudes. Walker says these shifts had bases that were partly legal (the ADEA amendment), partly technical (a national shortage of engineering talent), and partly attitudinal, with top management exhibiting a new response to the concept of hiring older workers.

The ten engineers all came in at the level of project engineer and above, with annual salaries of $25,000 or more. That means they are group leaders for major projects involving expenditures ranging from $100,000 to $1 million. None of these represent new plant construction, for which the company hires systems engineers on a consulting basis; rather they involve retrofit design and the replacement and integration of parts of existing systems, either because of technological improvement or obsolescence, or both. Since the engineers were hired for skills they already possessed, no training was needed. Walker and his management see them as potential long-service engineers. To make certain the company stays competitive, they are currently reviewing their compensation and benefit program in relation both to their area and to the industry as a whole.

Insurance Companies and Banks

SOUTHWESTERN LIFE INSURANCE COMPANY

Southwestern Life Corporation, with its wholly-owned subsidiary, Southwestern Life Insurance Company, is a nonfamily owned life insurance company in the state of Texas. It employs 1700 people in 35 states, 1000 at the home office in Dallas where the professional management staff and their clerical support number about 850. In addition, approximately 75 employees service and maintain the company-owned building.

Southwestern has a strong policy of internal promotion. All but executive job openings are posted and employees are free to bid for them. Many management jobs require professional credentials in the medical, legal, actuarial science, and data processing fields. Since most people come to the company in entry-level positions, one of personnel's major functions is employee development. The company hires and promotes according to ability. Robert Edwards, vice president for personnel, puts a high premium on maturity and experience, and the company advertises in newspapers which circulate in Dallas and ten cities within a 40-mile radius, as well as in a shopping newsletter that goes to 18,000 suburbanites. The ad suggests that individuals with rusty office skills consider coming to work at Southwestern. The company is prepared to help restore efficient performance.

In the last two years, 50 people over the age of 40 have been promoted to higher positions in the home office. Twenty-five moved from one level of nonexempt job to a higher level, while 13 stepped into management slots from nonexempt positions. Within the exempt category, 16 people moved to a higher management function, and of the total number promoted, 16 were male and 34 female.

One 41-year-old secretary at a branch office started up the promotional ladder by taking a job in sales, where her success led to a management assignment in the executive area of the home office. She is now a corporate officer. A 60-year-old woman in a general clerical job moved into a secretarial position. A 45-year-old female from the company's mortgage and real estate section landed a job as a conveyancer, which involves handling a series of complex contracts. A 54-year-old man went from a skilled offset press operator to unit leader; he had started with the company as an elevator operator. A 51-year-old who had started in the clerical area worked her way up to the level of junior officer, where she has the authority to sign official documents.

In the same two years Southwestern hired 60 people over the age of 40, the oldest of whom was 69. The average age of this group was 51 and all but 2 got full-time jobs. Their employment was across the board—in building services, clerical and secretarial work, and first- and second-level management slots. Salaries ranged from $7000 to $30,000 per year. And while the company's retired employees have so far shown little interest in returning to work, Southwestern tries to accommodate those who do, either in the clerical department or as consultants. Most recently they employed a retired attorney whose expertise was needed on a particular fraud claim.

BANKERS LIFE AND CASUALTY COMPANY

In early 1979, Bankers Life and Casualty Company, a Chicago-based company with 5000 home office and field employees, and 3000 field agents, established an in-house agency to employ retired Bankers' workers on a temporary or part-time basis. According to Dr. Anna Marie Buchmann, Bankers' human resources director, this "temporary workers pool" allows the company to obtain highly skilled workers without paying employment agency fees and permits annuitants to earn extra money and maintain a feeling of usefulness. Between March and November 1979 pool workers put in 1685 hours in clerical positions at wages which averaged $3.45 an hour. The company has saved nearly $3000 in agency fees.

Minnie Schenker, senior counselor in Bankers' human resources department, says she has 35 annuitants in the pool, 12 of whom are "extremely active." While some managers were initially apprehensive about bringing retirees back to work, their uneasiness has turned to delight over the "terrific job the retirees are doing," Schenker says. "And, because they know our company, they need virtually no time-consuming orientation."

Bankers Life is no stranger to the productive capacities of older workers. It has never had a mandatory retirement policy. This large company, with $1 billion in assets and $4 billion of in-force life insurance, simply sets performance standards for each job which become the only criteria for employment. Age analyses of their work force over the last 25 years have shown a remarkably constant percentage for workers over 50, 55, 60, and 65, the latter group holding steady between 3 and 4 percent. Says Bankers' president Robert P. Ewing, ". . . our experience shows it is bad business to exclude competent people from the work force on the basis of age alone. It is the myths about older workers that should be retired, not older workers."

The first myth, that voluntary retirement will lead to a top-heavy work force, has not happened at Bankers. While at least 70 percent of all workers reaching age 65 chose to stay on during the last five years, because of the departure of employees under 65, the proportion of older people has never exceeded 4 percent of the home-office staff of 4000 and 6.8 percent of their agents in the field. Moreover, most workers retire voluntarily by the age of 75. This finding supports the contention of Dr. K. Warner Schair, a University of Southern California gerontologist, who says, "if a chronologically meaningful retirement age were to be selected today, it would have to be made at least a decade later than would have made sense 20 years ago."

The second myth, that older workers have a significantly higher rate of absenteeism, was not borne out by a study Bankers did in 1977 which compared absentee rates of 128 workers under 65 with those of a control group over 65. Thirteen people under 65 had perfect attendance as compared with 34 in the over-65 sample. There was a much higher rate of half-day absences among younger workers (18 to 41), but this trend was gradually reversed in the 2- to 3-day absence range. An averaging out of absenteeism for the entire study produced an arithmetic mean for the under-65 sample of 5.3 days per employee, as compared to 7.5 days for the over-65 group. Long-term absences of 10 days or more occurred with the same frequency for both cohorts. Additional statistics for the first six months of 1979 showed that only 2 out of 274 on-the-job injuries involved older workers.

The third myth, that older workers are less productive, runs counter to Bankers' experience. Because productivity is their major guideline, performance appraisals are conducted every six months. Where slippage occurs, counseling with the supervisor or a personnel officer is usually instituted.

The fourth myth, that it is too costly to retain older workers, is not supported by Bankers' analysis. Frank Angerame, insurance and retirement consultant for the company, says that because workers over 65 are eligible for Medicare, Bankers' liability is actually reduced. It is more costly for them when a younger worker gets sick. As far as pensions are concerned, he points out that if the over-65 employee retires, "Bankers would be paying both pension benefits and the salary of the replacement. Added to that are the costs involved in training the new employee. It just has to be more economical to have a nonmandatory retirement policy."

Bankers not only retains its older workers, it hires individuals over 65 who have been forcibly retired by other companies. Herschel Bold started working at Bankers as a mail messenger in 1965 at age 68, after 42 years with the post office. Now in his eighties, he keeps in shape with daily calisthenics. Frances Stapleton was secretary to the president of another insurance company until her forced retirement at age 65. In five years with Bankers she has received three promotions and is secretary to a divisional director. George K. Morton came to the company in 1947 after 30 years with the federal government, where he was one of the original auditors with the IRS. Morton worked as a vault custodian until his death at the age of 89, rolling up a nearly perfect attendance record. Albert

Weinberg started with Bankers as an insurance agent and moved up through the sales department until he became assistant to the president. He retired at the age of 74 after pioneering the company's direct mail marketing program, which experienced record growth under his stewardship. Mary Rutledge received an appointment as a Bankers' agent in 1947, a position she held for 30 years. And for Harry Belkin, an agent at Bankers' Grand Rapids office, aging did not mean decreasing income. In 1976, at the age of 76, his earnings were the second highest of a group of 200 salesmen over the age of 64.

MORGAN GUARANTY TRUST COMPANY OF NEW YORK

This bank, with a work force of 10,000, averages 70 retirees annually. Approximately 50 annuitants are rehired every year, and each works an average of 30 days. They handle proxy work during a peak season which runs from January through April and also work in the collection department, where a large, seasonal bond-coupon volume builds up in January and July. During the summer months annuitants fill in for vacationing clerical staff. The bank hires its retirees selectively by department, keeping a file of productive ex-employees who have expressed a desire for part-time work. Annuitants keep their pensions and receive an hourly wage, free lunches, and the opportunity to participate in the bank's profit-sharing plan. Arthur T. Barkman, assistant vice-president, notices that the same people come back each year, but only for a two- to four-year period; by age 70 almost all have fully retired. Barkman, a 45-year veteran with Morgan Guaranty, had planned to retire early last year. A family illness made him change his mind; he was pleased that the bank suggested that he self-schedule his workweek, allowing him to meet his increased family responsibilities.

BANK OF AMERICA

Bank of America, with 75,000 employees and 1100 branches, is the largest bank in the world. As of January 1, 1979 it started hiring its own annuitants into part-time positions as tellers, clerks, and secretaries. A few are employed in a training capacity, teaching newer employees about jobs they themselves held for many years. All work 20 hours or less per week to protect their pension and Social Security income. A fledgling development, Bank of America has 70 annuitants currently employed on this program.

WESTERN SAVINGS AND LOAN ASSOCIATION

This small bank has 700 employees and 48 branches within the state of Arizona. The average age of its work force is 33 and the bank has only 4 bona fide retirees. However, they do hire annuitants and older people to staff their branches in peak business hours, at lunch time, during evenings and weekends. In the Sun City region of Maricopa County, where most residents are retired individuals, Western Savings and Loan branch employees are primarily senior citizens. Bill Candland, vice-president, employee relations, says they generally relate better to the customers than do younger workers.

Manufacturers

KUEMPEL CHIME CLOCK WORKS

Kuempel Chime Clock Works was founded in 1916 by Reuben Kuempel, father of the current president of the firm, Audrey McGregor. This small manufacturer of chime clock kits has always been a family business with a relaxed atmosphere which recognizes the individual needs of each worker. All current Kuempel employees are over 50, except Mary Jean McGregor, the firm's secretary-treasurer, who is a granddaughter of the founder. According to McGregor, the policy of hiring older workers "sort of evolved." Kuempel's oldest employee, now 92 and a skilled craftsperson who works on brass pendulums, was a self-employed auto mechanic until he retired in 1957. He started sharpening saws in his garage and one day wandered over to the nearby Kuempel plant to ask Reuben senior if he needed anything sharpened. They got to talking, Kuempel offered him a job and he has been there ever since. He still maintains his own home and drives a car.

McGregor says that the firm's history of hiring part-time workers and its policy of allowing workers to schedule their own time has produced an atmosphere conducive to older employees. She describes the staff as strongly motivated individuals. Many of the firm's 20 employees have simply "come through the door," having heard that Kuempel hires regardless of age. Some get their jobs strictly by chance. Two years ago a self-employed carpenter came in looking for a mantel clock, which Kuempel does not make. While there, he was offered work as a cabinetmaker. At 52, he was one of the firm's younger new-hires. Only once has a placement agency been involved. A social worker at the local Veterans Hospital placed a 50-year-old craftsperson with Kuempel several years ago. Of the remaining employees, five are in their seventies, seven in their sixties, and the rest are between fifty and sixty. "We don't have anyone in their eighties," said McGregor, wistfully. "I don't know why."

Four of the staff work full time, two in the office and two in production. Half the remaining employees work more than 20 hours a week. All production workers receive an hourly wage. Only full-timers are eligible for the company's profit-sharing, pension plan, medical and life insurance. Many of the workers are retired and receive Social Security. In the past they were post office employees, railroad workers, or salespeople. All have one thing in common: they like to work with their hands and have hobbies that employ this talent.

Training at Kuempel is informal and on-the-job. Someone who knows how to do something shows a new employee how. Since the basic clock movement is imported from Germany, the craftspeople at Kuempel are either adjusting the movement, making additional parts, or building the wooden cabinets or casings which house the clocks or the packaging needed for proper shipping. Most workers can do more than one job and they fill in for each other during illness or vacation. New workers either integrate quickly into the company "family" or terminate employment themselves. Flexible work and vacation schedules, and working at home when necessary, perhaps while caring for a sick spouse, have all been tried successfully by this small business.

There are no special, age-related problems for these workers. Normal eyeglasses suffice and no stronger magnification is needed to perform the required tasks. An annual brunch given by the McGregor family and periodic "pot luck" suppers help draw the work force into a comfortable unit. There is not much socializing off the job, according to McGregor, "but then again, they don't need that; they are having such a good time here at work."

FERTL, INC.

Hoyt Catlin, an 89-year-old Connecticut Yankee, founded Fertl in 1954 and is still its president. The company employs ten retired industrial workers whose average age is 72. The employees are referred by the Senior Personnel Placement Bureau of Norwalk, an operation started by local business leaders, including Catlin, to find jobs for the large pool of retirees in this manufacturing community. While the primary motivation for working is financial, with none of the employees having sufficient retirement income to manage in an inflationary economy, the workers here do not want to be idle and do enjoy feeling useful. Catlin, who has been working for 70 years himself, finds them a stable and reliable group, with a low rate of absenteeism and lateness. "There is no substitute for maturity," he says.

The product is Fertl-Cubes, a scientific soil substitute used to germinate garden seeds. One-eighth of a billion cubes have been sold in 25 years. "We've been successful," says Catlin. "We charge enough for the product to make a reasonable profit."

This was not always the case. Catlin originally imported the cubes from an English company which went out of business because selling them for 1¢ each proved unprofitable. He began manufacturing them here in 1956, using a formula devised by a friend with a Ph.D. in botany. He immediately raised the price. Today, two blocks of 20 cubes each sell for $3.10, and five blocks (100 cubes) sell for $5.75, the most popular package.

No particular skills are needed for this simple operation. On-the-job training consists of showing each worker what to do. The ingredients are placed in small cement mixers; the mixed, moist material is then processed into cubes in blocks of twenty. A worker transfers the cubes to racks where they are dried by an airstream for a day and a half. Other employees fill the preplanted cubes with seeds, or pack and label them; others work in the office. The jobs are interchangeable. All employees, except Catlin's second-in-command, are paid an hourly wage slightly higher than the legal minimum and usually work a 30-hour, 5-day week. They receive a monthly money bonus for regular attendance and a cash gift at Christmas. Levels of pay vary slightly with experience. There is no sick leave, pension or health insurance but workers get a prepaid vacation equal to 4 percent of their total annual wage, which usually translates into two weeks during the summer.

The atmosphere in the plant is harmonious and friendly. The most strenuous job, lifting the containers of wet material to the processing machines, was accomplished without undue effort by a male worker aged 74. Female employees do the less demanding packing and labeling. The workers' past employment history is varied, including all sorts of marginally paid manufacturing tasks. There is no hierarchy; rather, this is an extended family with Catlin serving as father figure. No formal, nonmonetary recognition system exists, and there is no problem with pilfering as workers can ask for and receive whatever products they want for their own use.

The employees live nearby, either alone or with spouses, and all but two drive themselves to work. There is little socializing off the job although there used to be when the operation was larger, particularly among the women. Only half the plant is utilized; production could be doubled if business warranted it.

Problems involved in hiring older workers can be obviated, according to Catlin, by adapting the operation to the slower pace of elderly people. Allowance must be made for weakened vision, reduced muscular potency, fatigue, and impaired resistance to infectious disease, particularly the common cold. The plant must be kept warm, workers cannot be pressured, and the more serene the atmosphere, the better the results.

Catlin's own background includes extensive experience in personnel work. He has been hiring people for 60 years. He spent 10 years building public utilities in Connecticut, the South, and the Far West, and has worked for General Foods, Westinghouse, and McGraw-Hill. For 5 years, from 1973 to 1978, Fertl was part of the Burpee Corporation, a division of General Foods, and Catlin ran it. During this period, there was no change in personnel policy.

Catlin, lively and energetic, has no plans to stop working. "We'll keep going as long as we get a return," he says. "As for retirement, hell no! I'm having the best time of my life. Too many acquaintances of mine have retired and in one way or another just died. Next spring I'm taking my fourth trip around the country, and I'm driving the whole way."

EVANS PRODUCTS

Evans is a conglomerate with 16,000 employees nationwide in 400 locations. These facilities are virtually autonomous. They make and lease railroad cars, manufacture custom homes and their components, are involved in lumbering operations, and maintain retail outlets which sell do-it-yourself building supplies. Annual sales are $1.5 billion. The company is headquartered in Portland, Oregon, with an executive and support staff of 250.

Evans hires workers regardless of age. At its Harbor Mill plant in Aberdeen, Washington, where plywood siding is manufactured, 15 percent of its 1979 hires were over 40. This small facility, employing 220 hourly and 32 salaried workers, has annual sales of $21 million. Skip Strait of the industrial relations department says the company finds older workers its most stable and reliable employees. "They have already grown up," says Strait, "you don't have to raise them." Management at Harbor Mill sees a new hire of age 40 as a potential long-service employee because the average retirement age of its work force is 62. A bidding system is in effect, and Strait notices that older production workers tend to "bid" for self-pacing jobs. One example is a "reworker," an employee who repairs faulty wood panels. "Reworkers" operate in teams of 2 and of the 12 currently employed, 10 are over 55. Another popular self-pacing job is operating the raiman machine, which patches wood veneer. Here 8 of the 10 raiman operators are over 40.

Similarly, at Evans' Corvales plant 85 miles south of Portland, where a staff of 400 manufacture hardboard, glass walls, and battery separators, workers over 40 are routinely hired because of their reliability. Of 20 machinists taken on in 1979, 8 were over 40. These workers operate punching, glueing, clipping, press, and board-printing machines. Annuitants are hired for temporary projects, either in construction jobs when Evans is building a new plant or expanding an existing one, or for major maintenance overhaul. Last year a retired millwright was brought back for a month to recondition an old machine. Most of these jobs do not exceed two to three months, and workers are hired on an hourly basis with no effect on their pensions. The majority of annuitants prefer to keep their postretirement earnings below the allowable limits of the Social Security law.

In the past the usual retirement age at the Corvales plant was 65. In 1979, Al Webb, director of personnel, found that all four employees reaching 65 were talking about staying on, citing inflation as the major reason. Jill Roake, personnel administrator at corporate headquarters, has observed a similar trend. Five of their staff are past 65, including the chief executive officer, the purchasing manager, two chief clerks and one salesperson, all of whom are working full time.

Five years ago the firm's payroll officer decided not to retire at 65, but asked that her job be redesigned for less responsibility. The company agreed, allowing her to handle the payroll for nonexempt workers. The duties involved in preparing the exempt payroll were given to the person slated to replace her. She is still working at age 70. Roake says the company would be glad to do the same for other employees, upon request.

AMALGAMATED CLOTHING AND TEXTILE WORKERS OF AMERICA

The Labor Bureau of the New York Joint Board, Amalgamated Clothing and Textile Workers of America, functions as the employment arm of the clothing industry in the metropolitan area, a responsibility it has taken over from the New York State Employment Division. They match job seekers with opportunities in 150 manufacturing and contracting concerns in New York City. There are more people looking for work than there are jobs in this shrinking industry, which suffers from seasonal fluctuations and foreign competition.

According to Morton Goldklang, director, the bureau is able to place retirees because they are skilled craft workers who can handle the complications of setting in place intricate parts of clothing. Sleeve setters, collar makers, and pocket makers have more of a chance of finding employment than do workers without these skills.

Goldklang expects to see fewer annuitants asking for work because of an anticipated change in the unemployment compensation law which will ban retirees from collecting unemployment compensation. At present, a retired worker can receive unemployment compensation after 20 weeks of covered employment.

Academia

UNIVERSITY OF CALIFORNIA, HASTINGS COLLEGE OF THE LAW

In 1974, Professor Richard R.B. Powell was voted "outstanding lecturer" by the students at Hastings in San Francisco. Nothing unusual, except that at the time, Powell was 84 years old.

Powell, a distinguished legal scholar, had taught for 38 years at Columbia Law School, until his forced retirement in 1959. There followed three years as visiting professor on the law faculties of Harvard, New York University, Boston College, Cornell University, and the University of Michigan. In 1962 he accepted a faculty appointment at Hastings, the country's second largest law school. Hastings was able to offer him a permanent spot because it has never had a policy of mandatory retirement. For the other schools, having a retired professor on staff for more than a semester or a year would have made it difficult to enforce retirement on the regular faculty.

Hastings' enlightened policy grew out of need, not dogma. A small, poor school in 1940, it could not afford to set up a retirement system for its own faculty. Dean David Snodgrass decided to turn this liability into an asset by offering employment to distinguished legal scholars who had been forced to step down elsewhere. Hastings soon acquired a prestigious group of legal educators, and by 1948 the board of directors made appointing retirees official policy. By 1974 the "65 club" of older faculty members comprised 50 percent of the staff.

According to Aletha Titmus Owens, Hastings' general counsel, that ratio dropped to 25 percent by 1979. Owens, a Hastings alumna, says that the older professors are well regarded by the students and respected by their colleagues. "Everyone wants to study with the people who wrote the textbooks," she remarked. "And you have to be a leader in your field to get an appointment here. It takes six to eight years to be awarded tenure and all professors are evaluated by their peers. It's a kind of super-recognition to be on this faculty."

Owens thinks the decreasing number of older professors has to do with Hastings' high standards and the fact that the Age Discrimination in Employment Act (ADEA), while exempting universities from the new mandatory retirement age of 70 until 1981, has set the stage for other schools to retain their talented teachers.

Hastings' annuitant-appointees keep their pensions from all previous employment. In addition to salary, they may participate in the school's Teachers Insurance and Annuity Association of America-College Retirement Equities Fund (TIAA-CREF) plan.

Professor Powell approved of mandatory retirement. In a 1974 interview he said, "It jars you out of a rut and often stimulates a new burst of energy. I favor the stimulation of institutions like Hastings, not only in law, but also in medicine, in theology, and in engineering, where those still able to do a good job of teaching can continue to do so."

6
Assessing and Advising

It is difficult to overestimate the importance of the American workplace in contemporary life. It is not just the area in which people earn a living, spend most of their time, and learn how to function within a deliberate and complex social structure. It is also the arena of professional development, where employers promise a certain amount of guidance and training, and employees put themselves on the line for judgment. Thus, the advisory function of the corporation, bank, utility, or government agency has significant impact. A single policy can take on vast importance when it is applied to hundreds or thousands of people.

This section deals with four forms of assessment and advice—performance appraisal, continuing education and training, occupational alcoholism programming, and preretirement counseling. Fifteen separate units are discussed—nine manufacturers of such disparate items as cereals, draperies, and aircraft, one government department, one major utility, two insurance companies, one bank, and one nonprofit national counseling service. The sizes of the organizations vary: three have fewer than 10,000 employees, nine fall between 10,000 and 100,000, one employs 120,000 people, and one, AT&T, has just over 1 million. Together these organizations represent a population of almost 2 million.

Performance Appraisal

Although it is generally recognized that performance appraisal systems are a conventional and necessary part of management strategy in the American business community, there is a wide disagreement about their methods and reliability. A recent Conference Board study of performance appraisal programs in 293 companies cites their cyclical record.

The history of performance appraisal in this country is characterized by the development and implementation of some new appraisal mechanism, a period of initial enthusiasm for it, followed by a period of deepening disillusionment as its problems became evident, and finally the development of some new mechanism that was supposed to solve the problems experienced with the old one. That process appears still to be under way. Over half the firms in the survey report that the systems they currently use have been developed within the last three years.*

The reactions of authorities, researchers, and corporate executives run the gamut of opinion from those who say that appraisals are counterproductive because they harass employees, to those who want to add more digits to the numerical rating scales in the quest for objectivity and accuracy.

Fact rather than opinion is affecting business attitudes toward appraisal systems. And in this case fact has to do with government rulings that performance appraisals are bona fide selection instruments which require validation and objectivity, and also with recent court decisions which insist that appraisal programs be "reasonable, relevant, and reliable."** According to Michael D. Batten, senior staff associate at the National Manpower Institute, the courts have generally upheld performace appraisal systems that are "comprehensive, rational, communicative, and fair."

The Age Discrimination in Employment Act (ADEA) adds another group of protected employees to those delineated by earlier civil rights legislation, and employers are looking anew at their appraisal programs in the light of that law.

The Conference Board survey found general agreement on the main purposes of performance appraisals. They provide feedback to employees, allow management to make decisions regarding salary and promotions, and identify developmental needs. Two-thirds of the personnel managers interviewed for the study approved of the systems currently in use in *their own* companies, and this approbation jumped to 90 percent

*Robert I. Lazer and Walter S. Wilkstrom. *Appraising Managerial Performance: Current Practices and Future Directions.* (New York: The Conference Board, 1977).

**James W. Walker and Daniel E. Lupton. "Performance Appraisal Programs and the Age Discrimination Law." *Aging and Work* (Spring 1978).

for programs developed within the last year.

But others question the accuracy of performance appraisals. Borman's research under controlled laboratory conditions found employee evaluations too unreliable.*   Nathan Winstanley, compensation research manager at Xerox and its resident expert, notes that appraisals are not very accurate. Using a complex statistical analysis, he finds that employee ratings, particularly in the middle of the scale, are "loaded with error" and cites more than 24 "non-performance variables" which have been found to decrease the accuracy of appraisals. He concludes that, since the research shows it is not possible to distinguish in the mid-range with precision "where most ratings are concentrated in the majority of U.S. organizations," the practical implication is clear: "Don't ask managers to measure what they cannot (or will not). At least, reduce the number of rating categories to three." In this recommendation, Winstanley is referring to administrative decisions involving salary and promotion. For a developmental-type appraisal, he opposes the use of any numbers at all and favors written reports.

Winstanley goes further. He says bluntly that if performance appraisals are not accurate and not subject to *meaningful* grievance procedures, the 30 million people subject to them are being deprived of "due process." He feels this civil liberties issue, which he calls "a public policy matter," should and will be addressed in the future.**

Regardless of whether accuracy is possible, it appears the active search for effective method will continue. One thing is clear. Current practice is moving in two definite directions—increasing the involvement of the appraisee in the evaluation process, and separating the appraisal of current performance from career development planning.

GRUMMAN AEROSPACE CORPORATION

At Grumman, performance appraisal is strictly a career-development tool and is separated from all compensation considerations. This is largely due to Daniel Knowles, Grumman's personnel director, who is philosophically opposed to tying raises and layoffs to the evaluation of employees.

---

*W. Borman. "Exploring Upper Limits of Reliability and Validity in Job Performance Ratings." *Journal of Applied Psychology* 63 (1978).

**Nathan Winstanley 1978: personal communication.

Performance ranking is used in these matters. Department supervisors are asked to rank employees in order of their usefulness to the unit. Who is most valuable in getting the work done? Who is expendable? Knowles says this is not a difficult determination at each end of the spectrum; the problem is in the middle. How do you differentiate between the eighteenth and nineteenth worker in a group of thirty? Knowles believes all forms of appraisal are subjective and is fond of quoting Douglas McGregor, father of the art, as saying that the best performance evaluation is a blank piece of paper.

Grumman is certainly familiar with the practice of performance ranking, since it was a major tool in the reduction in force triggered by drastic cuts in the nation's space program in the late sixties. Grumman's work force was cut almost in half over approximately a ten-year period by the reduction in force as well as by attrition. Still the largest employer on New York's Long Island, the corporation currently employs 20,000 people. Eleven thousand are professional and managerial; the remaining workers fall into white- and blue-collar categories.

Knowles's experience with performance-based ranking ten years ago was the beginning of his "age sensitivity." After the reduction in force, the average age of the company's work force jumped from 37 to 45, indicating that older workers had been the more productive. Knowles became interested in the relationship between productivity and aging, and, in 1973, began analyzing Grumman's work force by age and category. He has come to regard this procedure as an essential tool in planning, training, retention, and retirement strategies. Knowles is critical of the U.S. Department of Labor for not providing an age analysis of the national work force by occupation and skills so that a company can ascertain how its work force stacks up against national norms, in different classifications. Although he knows that 68 percent of Grumman's employees are over 40 as compared with the national average of 45 percent, he has no idea how his professional staff compares to national norms, because those figures do not exist. His prescription: a how-to-book for American industry which will provide a national demographic analysis by work categories and skills, eliminate myths about older workers, and convince corporations that it is good business to hire and retain older workers.

Grumman also uses performance ranking in its job-bidding procedure. All jobs through the first three supervisory levels for which no one is in line are subject to open competition through posting and bidding. It works as follows. The position of production control supervisor in department 6 opens up. Fourteen people apply for it. The department manager has to rank them, 1 through 14, using applicable experience, educational levels, and past job performance as guidelines. The manager chooses one candiate because that person's experience and education best fit the job. Other applicants come in second, third and fourth. Four applicants are judged completely unqualified. This analysis is then reviewed by the departmental promotion review board, composed of management people and the EEO officer. Their task is to scrutinize the objectivity of the selection process.

One key to effective performance ranking lies in sensitizing managers to the biases of age, sex, and race. At Grumman this is accomplished with a four-hour segment on affirmative action which is part of all supervisory development seminars. Knowles believes that age bias is perhaps the most rampant and insidious of all because it is often unconscious. Formal training is therefore reinforced by off-the-cuff meetings between members of the personnel team and the supervisory staff.

The career-development aspect of performance appraisal is carried out six months before or after salary is discussed. The feedback in this session is in the nature of constructive criticism from the supervisor to the worker, with developmental needs a primary concern. For example, an assembler-riveter who cannot read a blueprint takes a blueprint-reading course; an engineer with strong technical skills who is unable to make a coherent presentation at a meeting is sent for training in leadership skills; a supervisor who has trouble getting along with people needs a seminar in interpersonal relations.

The fact that developmental needs are addressed according to need and ability and are not hampered by age bias is strongly supported by statistical evidence. At Grumman, 83 percent of officials and managers, 70 percent of professional employees, and 66 percent of the technical staff are over 40. Says Knowles, "You can be sure they did not get there without training."

THE KELLOGG COMPANY

In the past year Kellogg has completely revised its approach to performance appraisal, going to an open system where employees have free access to their files and ratings. One impetus for the change was a Michigan law mandating employee access; the other was a need to standardize performance evaluations among various departments.

The new method involves breaking the appraisal into four components. The first identifies common key areas for all jobs. They are quantity, quality, knowledge of the requirements of the job, technical competence, interpersonal relations, managerial skills, and reliability. Individual supervisors may add to this basic outline any aspects of performance they consider relevant to a specific job. Part two involves identifying trouble spots and finding ways to improve and correct them. The third aspect concerns the need for dialogue between the employee and the supervisor, so that workers know where they fit into the department and the organization, where they are now, where they want to go, and how they are going to get there. A standard question for this part of the assessment might be, "What do you want to be doing in five years?" The final component involves the employee's perception of the appraisal—whether the employee agrees with the supervisor and thinks the appraisal is fair and accurate. Where an employee does not, a written statement by the employee is permitted and further discussion may be initiated with the personnel department.

To implement this policy, Kellogg has established performance review seminars for managers. The first group accommodated 25 supervisors and was so well received that the company quickly ran four more seminars of four hours each. These begin with a talk by David Wallridge, manager of organization planning, giving the background of the changes in performance appraisal: the legal mandate, the fact that it is now company policy to use this approach in employee evaluation, the belief that it is good business and serves as an important tool in future organization planning. He describes the open access system, the need for objectivity, and then discusses performance and personal skills assessment. The last part of the seminar is devoted to a practice session and uses simulated interviews to demonstrate how to do it, the flow and pace, and what not to do.

BANKERS LIFE AND CASUALTY COMPANY

When this Chicago-based company decided to revise its performance appraisal, the purpose was threefold: to establish better communications between worker and supervisor, to permit more upward mobility, and to give employees a voice in their future career goals. That was in 1976. The new form traveled through all levels of management, finally surfacing for a trial run in late 1979. Two hundred employees and their supervisors were part of this pilot, which was used to develop a company-wide management training module to be used in 1980.

The new system, which replaces a one-sheet numerical point system unilaterally completed by the supervisor, retains objective measurements of attendance, punctuality, quantity and quality of work against a given standard. It adds two forms of goal setting, one for current performance, a second for future aims. It also adds feedback, so that employees know how well (or poorly) they are doing and what measures of a corrective or an improvement nature need to be taken before the next biannual evaluation. It allows the appraisee to attach comments to the form and request a review by the next level of management.

In dropping the numerical rating in favor of a written statement about job performance, this system asks the supervisor to consider such factors as job knowledge, judgment, comprehension, attitude, dependability/reliability, initiative, problem solving, adaptability, effort, efficiency, and communication. While most of these were rated on the old form, the last four are new additions to the performance appraisal equation.

People in the pilot study gave overwhelming approval to the employee-manager dialogue but some had problems with the goal-setting portion of the process. Many workers found it hard to articulate goals and some, particularly long-service employees at the top of their salary range, found them meaningless, especially if they had no wish to advance to the next level of responsibility. The overall reaction was favorable, however, and management feels that the problems revealed would be addressed in the training process. Howard Futterman, compensation manager at Bankers, says the appraisal procedure retains objectivity while permitting significant employee input regarding career development.

The supervisory training module is a two-day seminar. The first half-day deals with the philosophy of appraisals, why they are needed and what was expected to be achieved. The remainder is devoted to gaining an understanding of the new form, devising ways of dealing with goal-setting problems, and giving demonstrations of employee-supervisor exchanges, different styles of communicating, and ways of helping workers with their developmental planning. The seminar uses case histories, a specially prepared film, role playing, and group discussions. The goal-setting portion distinguishes four aims: correction, improvement, and innovation. The latter include taking on outside or supervisory responsibilities and embrace the long-range, developmental objectives of the appraisal process.

THE MEAD CORPORATION

The Mead Corporation is a decentralized company primarily in paper and forest products. It has approximately 150 locations worldwide. Individual units have considerable autonomy in managing their performance appraisal processes. Corporation guidelines suggest that: performance reviews be held at least once a year; employees have access to information used for performance appraisal; the criteria used be job related; and appraisals be written, and signed by two levels of supervision.

A performance appraisal training course has been developed by the Mead Development Institute, the company's in-house managerial training department. It is an intensive two-phase seminar which is conducted at the request of Mead operating units. The first part is devoted to the negotiated process by which supervisor and employee set job standards, using a performance negotiation worksheet. This identifies key elements of the job and establishes precise goals which can be expressed in measurable ways. Phase two deals with feedback mechanism—how both positive and negative data are constructively transmitted to the appraisee. The course uses role-playing, modeling, sample interviews, and tapes. The second phase identifies the different styles which managers use in relating to others and relaying information. The idea is to illustrate what works and what does not, and to help supervisors learn how to develop and manage a feedback style that is effective for them. About twenty people attend each phase of the seminar, which is given as often as necessary to accommodate the expressed needs of Mead units.

Kent Bradshaw, consultant with the institute, says that some managers find the goal setting "cumbersome" and initially struggle with its implementation. That has led the institute to consider ways of improving the process. It is examining assessment centers, competency modeling, and methods of job analysis, but has not yet decided on any new directions.

CONNECTICUT GENERAL LIFE INSURANCE COMPANY

In 1973, Connecticut General adopted a two-pronged performance appraisal system that separated the evaluation of the current job from the developmental appraisal. The first part of the system involves a joint evaluation of job performance by employee and supervisor using objective criteria. Multiple meetings are held during the year, the first to define objectives, the subsequent ones at 3, 7, and 12 months to review progress toward meeting them. These appraisals are in writing, providing automatic documentation and feedback. This part of the process is used to determine salary.

The developmental appraisal is held two months after the first performance appraisal conference. In the company view, this part of the process belongs to the employees. It is an opportunity to explore their developmental needs and interests, which can be in the current job or a different one, and draw up a plan to address those needs. For example, someone in a technical job who decides on a managerial career and gets the supervisory green light could go into a management training course, or take on the direction of a task force, or both. Another dimension of the developmental appraisal is that it provides management with an automatic skills bank and becomes a human resources tool for replacement strategy.

Each of the company's seven divisions has a personnel director who makes sure that the interviews take place. This process applies to 12,000 of the company's 14,000 employees. For workers in salary ranges below $10,000 a year a similar system with fewer meetings is in effect.

Donald Illig, director of compensation and benefits, who has been involved with the system since its inception and has watched various levels fall into place, feels it is working well. The move toward objectivity makes it easier for managers to be honest and not hide behind a kind of "nice guy" leniency. Earlier systems tended to judge people as individuals, so that criticism was taken personally and therefore often avoided. "As systems become more objective," says Illig, "there will be greater accuracy."

Continuing Education and Training

Although continuing education and training are a way of life in most large American corporations, and markedly so in high technology industries, the transfer of technical skills from retiring workers to their younger counterparts is a problem looking for a solution. There is not enough design work in the aerospace industry today for engineers to acquire the kind of expertise that was available to the generation trained during World War II or at the height of the space program. For example, Lockheed has not designed a new landing gear since completing work on the L-1011 ten years ago.

Howard Lockwood, corporate director of management development at Lockheed, believes the universities could fill this gap, incorporating more practical design work into their engineering schools. He thinks it would be possible to utilize older and/or annuitant engineers to staff such programs. The only other solution, says Lockwood, is in-house training in simulated projects, but these do not get off the ground because "not enough time and effort goes into technological transfer between experienced people and those coming in."

John Richardson, vice-president of industrial relations at Northrop Corporation, manufacturers of aircraft, electronic equipment, and computers, is also concerned about revitalizing vocational training. Northrop personnel visited over three dozen junior colleges and vocational schools and discovered that they were doing virtually nothing to train people in the critical area of machine tooling. Richardson points out that the aircraft industry today is moving away from labor-intensive work and into the use of sophisticated machinery in manufacturing. The problem for the schools in this type of training is the cost of the machinery; the problem for the companies is that, while they have the equipment, it is needed for production practically around the clock.

Dr. Paul Doigan, manager of technical recruiting for the General Electric Company, has similar concerns. GE sponsored a national industry education conference in early 1979 to improve the interaction between industry and academia and enhance career development opportunities for engineers. They brought together 64 engineering department chairmen, deans, and faculty members and an equal number of GE engineers for a series of dialogues on the current relationship between the business community and universities. Part of the problem, says Doigan, is that the people who are doing the teaching have never been in industry and do not understand its needs. On the other hand, top industrial engineering personnel cannot take off a semester or a year to teach. They lose too much because of the swift pace of technological development. Doigan, who served on the evaluation committee of the career facilitation programs sponsored by the National Science Foundation, thinks such programs can be used in high-technology industries to upgrade labor-force skills. "After all," observes Doigan, "that 25 percent dip in the 18-year-old age group is only ten years away. Companies like GE will not be able to get the work done without relying on people working longer." And "people working longer" in the technological sector of American industry means training.

According to William Grogan, dean of undergraduate studies at Worcester Polytechnic Institute, one of the motives behind the restructuring of the school's academic year in 1973 was the possibility of improving the two-way flow between industry and academia in time periods shorter than the standard semester. Worcester invited 12 companies to a conference to explore the idea that corporate personnel could afford seven weeks away from their jobs, either for upgrading their skills as students, or passing them on as teachers. Originally enthusiastic, most companies did not follow through. Grogan says the original acceptance of the concept came from the high-level managers who attended the conference. Further down the ranks, among the people who would actually participate, the program became harder to implement. Grogan feels this kind of activity does not receive the same recognition within industry that staying put and getting promoted does.

Bell Laboratories, the research and development arm of AT&T, has had an active partnership with many universities for years. Under a variety of arrangements Bell personnel regularly take off a semester or a year to teach engineering courses at universities and colleges with predominantly black student bodies. The company pays these employees their regular corporate salaries. Bell has another program of sponsored teaching where individuals work and teach part-time; it also grants about 12 sabbaticals annually to personnel who join a university's staff and payroll for a semester or academic year. Professors also spend their sabbaticals at Bell under a joint procedure by which they receive a temporary corporate appointment and the normal accompanying salary.

This is not to say that extensive educational opportunities do not exist inside the corporation. Almost every company contacted for this study offers managerial and technical training at universities, and tuition rebates, in addition to extensive in-house opportunities for upgrading skills and learning new ones. IBM has developed one of the most extensive corporate education programs in the country. More than 5000 part- and full-time instructors give courses in management development, technical updating, and job retraining. Of its total work force, which now numbers 180,000, more than 170,000 put in an average of 40 class hours each year, or close to 7 million student hours in all.

At Lockheed, with its smaller labor force of 60,000, there were 2000 enrollments in college classes in 1978, 170 people working toward master's degrees, 1700 in management training classes, 9000 in technical training classes, and 20 in university executive training institutes. In 1979 another 40 employees attended the company's newly established one-week executive institute.

GENERAL ELECTRIC COMPANY—
AEROSPACE ELECTRONIC SYSTEMS DEPARTMENT

Because design technology in the electronics field has changed dramatically, going from the use of analogue to digital technique, many older engineers find their skills outdated. To rectify this, Forrest Cooper, Jr., manager of engineering at GE's Aerospace Electronic Systems Department in Utica, New York, set up a retraining program in 1977 to teach long-service design engineers the newer method. This is in line with company policy which favors retraining to upgrade skills. Cooper calls it a "technical renewal program" to bring older engineers up to the level of design expertise of today's engineering graduates.

Two courses with 20 engineers each have been completed since the summer of 1977. The average age of the participants was over 40. During the 12-week program, which is the equivalent of three college credits, participants spent half of their workday in class and the other half at their regular jobs. The courses were developed and taught by graduates of the Advance Technical Course, GE's intensive three-year training program at the graduate level in mechanical, electrical, and nuclear engineering. While the participants were initially resistant to retraining, they found the course stimulating and are now pleased with the new technique. Cooper plans to continue the program, claiming that at least 40 more engineers in his department need this form of continuing education. He has sent a report on the pilot program to corporate headquarters because he believes the model has other applications within the organization.

THE INTERNATIONAL SILVER COMPANY AND
THE TRADE ADJUSTMENT ASSISTANCE ACT

The Trade Act of 1974 was passed to provide help for American workers adversely affected by foreign competition. Data through July 31, 1979 show that 466,923 workers who have lost their jobs because of imports have received $738,443,092 in benefits; 16,518 workers have entered training programs; 2389 have received a job-search allowance; another 1534 have had financial help with relocation; and 16,244 have been placed in new jobs.

The case involving the International Silver Company (INSILCO) of Meriden, Connecticut illustrates how jobs can be saved when government, private industry, and labor unions cooperate with TRAA to address economic dislocations. The circumstances first came to the attention of the Commerce Labor Adjustment Action Committee (CLAAC) as a result of Commerce Department efforts to mitigate the effects of import competition on the stainless steel/flatware industry.

The Washington representative of the United Steelworkers of America brought two officials of the Steelworkers' Meriden local to CLAAC to explain that competition from imports had cut deeply into domestic production. As a result, INSILCO, whose work force numbers 8000, was considering a major layoff that was expected to begin with 60 to 70 workers and to include an additional 350 later on. The average age of the threatened workers was 56, their average length of service, 20 years.

The CLAAC Secretariat suggested the possibility of retooling the plant and retraining the workers under the trade act to produce jet engine components. Strong demand for such capacity exists in the central Connecticut area as a result of a contract between the Boeing Company and the Pratt and Whitney Company to produce 80 new wide-bodied, medium-range passenger planes.

INSILCO's business planning manager initiated a dialogue, and a working relationship between the management of Pratt and Whitney and

INSILCO followed. INSILCO converted its stainless steel flatware production facility into a new tube-bending operation to supply aircraft engine and other industries. Their existing tool shop was turned into a general tooling business, and, with $170,000 in trade act funds, an apprenticeship training program was established, which has since been taken over by the state of Connecticut.

The 16-week training program consists of two classes of 20 workers each, all of whom are learning the demanding tool-and-die-making skill, one that takes approximately four years to master completely. This craft requires mathematical knowledge and the ability both to handle precision tools and read shop sketches. Previously these workers were machinists, buffers, and drop hammer operators. The course is taught by a master tool-maker, who is assisted by an overall apprentice instructor and an INSILCO retiree, a former tool-and-die maker, who helps with the practical machine instruction. Participants receive a training salary of $5.60 an hour.

The program is getting high marks from those involved with it. The assistant director of the Connecticut office of job training and skill development calls it highly successful and says participants are learning quickly. John Sartori of the Steelworkers local agrees, and William Groben, INSILCO's vice-president of manufacturing, points out that the new work reduced the extent of the projected layoffs. William Batt, executive secretary of CLACC, says this experience shows how trade readjustment assistance can be used creatively with tripartite cooperation.

AT&T

AT&T, with its 21 operating telephone companies, constitutes the largest utility company in the nation and employs just over one million workers. Each operating telephone company has a company-wide, as well as an inter-company, employee-initiated program of job transfer for all non-management categories including operators, clerical workers, craft, service, and sales personnel. It affects literally thousands of people.

The upgrade and transfer system has two parts. Part one deals with the transfer plan and with "job briefs," which describe the major functions of such positions as installation or repair technicians, frame attendants, and PBX installers. Besides highlighting the requirements of each job, the briefs list basic qualifications needed to fill those jobs, as well as additional factors, such as experience, training, special skills, and present job performance, which are taken into account in the candidate selection process. The process is not age sensitive so age is not considered.

The second part deals with the training function that goes with each job. This can be either classroom or on-the-job training (OJT), or a combination of both. All job briefs carry an affirmative action job classification and associated with each job is a time-on-location and a time-on-title requirement. This means that an individual taking advantage of the upgrade and transfer program and moving into a new position after training must stay with it for a given period of time before requesting another transfer. The time requirements vary from 6 to 30 months depending on the length of training. A high craft job with a 26-week training period would carry a 30-month proviso.

The system works this way. An employee fills out a form requesting transfer. Job briefs are readily available. All supervisors have access to them and the company publishes a booklet telling employees where else they can be found. In addition, supervisors are required to review the transfer plan and associated job briefs with their employees every year.

The request is evaluated by the upgrade and transfer bureau, staffed by the personnel department. They consider such items as attendance, current job performance, and the applicant's background as it relates to the job being requested. All approved transfer requests are then filed. When a job requisition comes through, the file is activated and a candidate is selected by the upgrade and transfer bureau.

Frequent transfer requests come from operators who want to become installation technicians, a position that pays about $100 more a week. Accepted applicants enter a 40- to 50-hour training course where they learn how to climb a telephone pole. They are also trained to take phones apart, wire the connections, run inside wiring in a home or business, and read service orders. Since the consent decree which AT&T signed with the government in 1973, the climbing course has been redesigned to accommodate women. A shoulder strength test has been added to the application procedure, since the female torso is not as strong as the male's, and the pole-climbing portion has been reduced to four hours a day, with the afternoon spent in class. Some tools have also been scaled down to reflect the smaller hand and arm spans of women. And learning to drive a van has been added to the curriculum.

Some technical jobs require longer training periods. A switching technician has to learn about electronic equipment and trains for three to four months. This job is comparable in level and pay to a computer technician. Other positions are testing technician, assignment technician, and frame attendant. All of these are inside jobs.

While company-wide age data are not available, AT&T has been keeping the government informed about its affirmative action program for women. These statistics show that while only one-twentieth of all installers are women, some are over 40. For example, in one operating telephone company, statistics indicate that 8 percent of the female installers of business equipment are between 40 and 45, while in another operating company 14 percent of the female installation technicians are between the ages of 41 and 65.

THE MEAD CORPORATION

This diversified corporation, with headquarters in Dayton, Ohio, manages a variety of businesses—principally paper and forest products, but also including castings, distribution services, rubber products, packaging, coal, and advanced information-retrieval and reproduction systems. Annual sales are $2.3 billion and the work force numbers 17,000 hourly employees and 8,000 salaried employees. There are more than 150 operating locations scattered throughout the world.

The Mead Development Institute is the managerial training arm of the company. A professional staff of three, plus two support personnel, and augmented by faculty drawn from local universities, conducts 40–50 courses every year. Some courses are developed in-house while others are purchased "off-the-shelf" from outside sources or adapted from outside programs. The institute offerings reach about 600 employees annually.

There are two ways into the institute. Employees may apply, or managers may recommend specific courses to individuals, either to improve their job performance or to ready them for their next career step. Each year the staff develops a descriptive package which is sent to managers at all company locations.

The institute charges units for participation and monitors the curriculum, using participant evaluations, follow-up checks, and cost-per-student data. Those courses which are not well attended are dropped or revised. Thomas H. Schumann, Mead's director of selection and placement, stresses that the institute is not only for outstanding performers, but is used also to define and correct employees' weaknesses that show up during annual performance appraisals.

Mead Development Institute courses cover many topics. Some of the most popular focus on supervisory skills, decision making, business and report writing, and leadership—motivation. This latter program explores how various leadership modes affect people and how good matches between people and jobs can improve motivation and performance.

For example, one woman working in a personnel administration assignment was recommended for the leadership—motivation course. There she learned why she was not satisfied in her current job: she lacked the optimum motivational profile and interests. After discussions with her supervisor, she requested a transfer to a marketing division where her skills are being more productively utilized.

The institute offers one course on how paper products are manufactured and another in financial training for nonfinancial managers, where participants learn how to read financial reports and profit and loss statements. There is also a course in sales management and an intensive program dealing with performance appraisals.

In addition to the Mead Development Institute, the company has a tuition rebate program, which pays 75 percent of the tuition costs for any active employee who obtains supervisor approval to take job-related courses. The company will consider a leave of absence upon request from an employee for special circumstances, but this is rarely done.

For high potential managers, the corporation provides advanced management training at universities. About 12 people each year go to Harvard, MIT, Stanford, University of Chicago, or the University of Virginia to attend these advanced executive development programs.

At the most senior levels, executives take specialized leadership programs offered by a variety of schools and consulting firms. In all, Bradshaw, consultant with the institute, estimates that 9 percent of the entire work force takes advantage of some form of continuing education each year. The entire age spectrum is represented, including older workers, who most commonly cluster in the middle and higher management brackets.

Occupational Alcoholism Programming

There is wide agreement that alcoholism is a significant medical problem in the United States. The Third Special Report to the U.S. Congress on Alcohol and Health, prepared by the National Institute on Alcohol Abuse and Alcoholism (NIAAA) in June 1978, states:

It is estimated that there are 9.3 to 10 million problem drinkers (including alcoholics) in the adult population, or 7 percent of the nation's 145 million adults (18 years and older). This estimate includes both those who are alcoholic and those who are otherwise disabled as a result of alcohol. An estimated 10 percent of the adult male population and 3 percent of the adult female population are problem drinkers. Of the total adult problem-drinking population, 24 percent are female. This estimate is probably low because alcohol problems are manifested somewhat differently among women than among men, and prevalence estimation methodology historically has not accounted for this. Furthermore, some studies have suggested one-third of the problem drinking population is female.

Is alcoholism a disease of the older worker? The answer seems to be yes. The first obvious fact is that, because it takes many years for the effects of alcohol abuse to appear, its victims by definition have to be older people. But harder data exist. There is not only a significant increase in problem drinking in women, but the NIAAA report says "among married women under 65, those who are working have higher rates of heavier and problem drinking than those who are not employed outside the home, regardless of socioeconomic status." The most recent survey conducted in 1977 by Alcoholics Anonymous (AA), which now has more than one million members worldwide, shows that 85 percent of a sample of 15,000 AA members in the United States and Canada are over 30, and 35 percent of these are over 50. And the NIAAA report states flatly, "Evidence from epidemiologic research indicates that chronic, damaging drinking occurs throughout American society, and the greatest amount occurs among employed persons and their families." Finally, NIAAA notes that the 1976 Executive Caravan Survey showed "increased rates of heavier drinking among executives in private corporations, and pointed to the potential impact of drinking on responsible decision making."

In response to the problem, occupational alcoholism programming as a method of early identification and intervention is gaining greater acceptance. Between 1950 and 1973 the number of occupational alcoholism programs in the country jumped from 50 to 500. The big push, however, came in the mid-seventies. By 1977, 2400 organizations—2000 in private industry, the rest in the public sector—had started to work on this problem. The current trend is to place occupational alcoholism programs in personnel, industrial relations, or employee benefits divisions, rather than in medical departments as was true in the past. Unions are overcoming earlier resistance and taking an active part in expanding this service to affected workers. There is general agreement that the role of the supervisor is crucial in confronting employees with impaired performance, although diagnosis of alcoholism must be made by a qualified professional.

Most important, the NIAAA notes that "a substantial majority—72 percent—of executives among 'Fortune 500' companies with occupational programs believe that their organizations have saved money as a result of their companies' programs. A positive assessment of program effectiveness in overcoming job impairment due to alcohol use was almost universal among this group." NIAAA also notes that a number of groups have not been touched by occupational programs. Among them are small business, upper echelon executives, professionals, and persons working in isolated occupational settings.

GRUMMAN AEROSPACE CORPORATION

Grumman's commitment in this area is very strong, according to Daniel Knowles, director of personnel, who sees alcoholism in his company primarily as a disease of the middle-aged worker. Every Wednesday night the assistant director of the Long Island Council on Alcoholism conducts a session on alcohol abuse which several hundred people attend. The company has held two major seminars for its 2000 supervisors—the first, an orientation to the problem of alcoholism, the second involving diagnosis and treatment. Together they total four hours of lectures on the subject. Their purpose is to make the supervisory staff conscious of management's responsibility for corrective action and to give them the tools to take this action. The thrust is in keeping the issue focused on employee performance, getting help from the personnel department, and making the proper referrals to the medical department. Medical and personnel staff work closely together, and one member of the personnel department has had extensive training in alcoholic counseling. However, the company offers only regular or crisis intervention and referral, but no continuing therapy.

Referrals are made to the Long Island Council on Alcoholism, the Freeport, South Oaks, or Brunswick hospitals, or to AA, a psychiatrist, or clergyman. Grumman's major medical policy covers alcoholism so that funding for treatment is not a problem. This is in line with recent changes in funding patterns. While 25 percent of all Blue Cross plans specifically excluded alcoholism in 1972, by 1976 only 4 out of 60 plans responding to a survey excluded treatment for alcoholics. And, according to NIAAA, increasing numbers of private insurance carriers are providing coverage. Twenty states have enacted legislation which either mandates alcoholism coverage or requires that it be available as an option. There is indication that providing such coverage is cost effective in the long run. Preliminary findings from a California experimental project indicate that the average monthly nonalcoholism health care costs for both the alcoholic and the immediate family were reduced by 25 percent after the individual went into treatment for alcoholism.

There is a follow-up AA group within the Grumman organization which keeps an eye on recovered alcoholics. While not a spy system, it is sensitive to emerging problems in this special population. Knowles believes the workplace provides, in the last analysis, the most effective opportunity for corrective action.

ALCOHOL AWARENESS PROGRAM—U.S. DEPARTMENT OF STATE

Government statistics indicate that 6 percent of the national work force have a problem with alcoholism. To deal with this, Congress passed Public Law 91-616 in 1970, establishing an alcoholism treatment program in every government agency.

The State Department program, available to all of its 24,000 employees, consists of information, early detection, treatment, and rehabilitation. The information aspect consists of lectures, seminars, and presentations at all department meetings, overseas embassies, and the 16 courses given at the Foreign Service Institute. A film made specifically for the department is shown and a monthly article appears in the department newsletter. Everyone, from ambassadors to janitors, is included in this information barrage.

Detection of alcoholism is the responsibility of the supervisor, and the single criterion is job performance—whether the employee is late or absent too frequently or performs inadequately. Employees are referred to the departmental physician, who makes a diagnosis and, if necessary, refers the patient to a selected treatment center for a four-week treatment program. This includes an explanation of the physical, mental, and psychological aspects of alcoholism. Patients are exposed to AA, which is the primary outpatient referral service for continuing treatment.

The 80 State Department physicians and nurses receive special training at the Long Beach Naval Hospital in California. There, in a two-week course run by alcoholism authority Dr. Joseph A. Pursch, they learn about alcoholism as a disease. The department reports an 88-percent success rate and offers this program to its annuitants as well as to current staff and dependents.

Preretirement Planning

Increasingly, private industry is accepting the concept that helping employees plan for their retirement is a legitimate personnel function. A 1977 study conducted by The Conference Board, an independent, non-profit research organization with a 60-year history in the fields of business economics and business management, found that 88 percent of 800 corporations surveyed provided some sort of preretirement assistance to their workers.* The organizations studied included a wide variety of manufacturing companies in the fields of apparel and textiles, chemicals, building supplies, electronics, machinery, mining, paper, petroleum, publishing and printing, pharmaceuticals, tobacco, and transportation equipment, as well as banks, insurance companies, and public utilities. Of the 800 organizations, 572 had fewer than 5000 employees, 171 were in the 5000 to 25,000 range, and 57 were corporations with staffs of 25,000 and more; the largest employed 196,000 people. The 96 companies who furnished no preretirement assistance either did not offer their employees

---

*J. Roger O'Meara. *Retirement: Reward or Rejection?* (New York: The Conference Board, 1977).

pension protection or had such young work forces that the issue had not yet emerged. These findings compare with a 1964 Conference Board study which showed that only 65 percent of 974 participating companies were involved in preretirement programs.

The survey revealed two basic approaches to preretirement assistance. One provides financial information about company benefits and Social Security, while the second includes counseling in such areas as health care, the use of leisure time, legal matters, second careers, life-style adjustments, house arrangements, and financial planning. The Conference Board found that 371 of its respondents gave their employees only financial information, 170 firms added material about health insurance and Medicare, and 163 went into more detailed communication. Of this latter group, 60 companies supplied written information, 103 used some form of personal meeting, but only 12 concerns dealt with all seven areas. A number of personnel directors felt there was some danger in getting too involved in assessing and advising because of staff limitations, cost to the company, and the possible repercussions from former employees should the advice turn out to be faulty. Others recognized that there are good reasons for providing this service. It can reinforce retiring employees' morale and productivity, help recruit and retain dependable, high-quality staff, improve relations with unions, fulfill the company's social responsibilities, and enhance its public image.

A much smaller study conducted in 1978 by professors at Rutgers University and the University of Nebraska also found preretirement programs on the upswing. The professors, however, were critical of what they felt was the limited content of these programs, which focused too narrowly on financial matters to the exclusion of "the ego needs" of individuals who are changing roles in society, with the inevitable loss of peer-group association and identity. Recognizing that lack of money, time, and staff, and the fear of invading employee privacy, influence and restrict the scope of industry programs, these academicians favor an economic analysis and a modeling of costs of more sophisticated, problem-oriented counseling, on the grounds that the expense might be "offset by the improved effectiveness of the preretirees once their anxieties are reduced."*

*Sidney R. Siegel and Janet M. Rivas. "Characteristics of Existing and Planned Preretirement Programs." *Aging and Work* (Spring 1978).

AIM

AIM—Action for Independent Maturity—is the preretirement branch of the American Association of Retired Persons (AARP), a nonprofit, nonpartisan organization with over 12 million members. In 1971 AIM started developing materials on various aspects of retirement planning for its targeted age group of 50 to 65. By 1974 a packaged seminar program of eight sessions was introduced which covered the challenge of retirement, health and safety, housing and location, legal affairs, attitude and role adjustments, the meaningful use of time, sources of income, and financial planning. This was offered to employers and included a presentation kit containing guides for the administrator of the program and the discussion leader, participant manuals, review books, and filmstrips. The format of each session, which is designed to accommodate 20 to 25 people, uses advance reading, presentation of the above materials, case histories to encourage discussion, and follow-up exercises to be completed at home. In addition, each seminar participant receives a complimentary one-year membership in AIM, including a subscription to the magazine *Dynamic Years,* 12 retirement planning guides, and access to special pharmacy, motor club, and other services.

AIM has developed a five-day training program for personnel administrators and other professionals, offering 20 or more of these programs each year at various locations around the country. In 1978 the organization added a lecture series designed to reach large groups of between 50 and 500 people. This series has been used by government agencies, community colleges, and large service organizations. AIM maintains four regional offices in New York, Chicago, Long Beach (California), and Washington, D.C., the site of its national headquarters. Its staff of 35 develops all materials, and services the membership, which now numbers nearly 500,000 still-employed people in their middle years. More than 1600 corporations, educational institutions, government agencies, and other organizations have purchased AIM's services since 1971.

LEVI STRAUSS AND COMPANY

The world's largest apparel manufacturer has only about 700 retirees, yet it has been researching preretirement programs since 1977, because an age analysis of the work force, which numbers over 40,000 people, indicates that there will be 400 annuitants by 1985 and double that number by 1990. The company has an extensive program of benefits for retired employees.

Levi Strauss, which was founded in 1850 as a small family business, has grown geometrically in the last seven years and now has 63 production locations around the country and 5 regional distribution centers in Arkansas, Nevada, Texas, and Kentucky. Headquartered in San Francisco, where a staff of 3000 is employed, Levi Strauss has annual sales of over $2.0 billion.

In 1978 the company decided to try the AIM program on an experimental basis and, after sending members of its personnel department to an AIM training seminar, ran 200 employees through the program during 1979. Maureen E. Veach, manager of retirement services, calls the program excellent but says it is too broadly based for the company's needs. For example, an approach which goes heavily into financial planning is not appropriate for a company like Levi Strauss, with a large nonexempt production staff. The company's substantial sales force, with jobs which require extensive travel, may need a heavy emphasis in their preretirement planning on time management and interpersonal relations. Another consideration was the use of material that could easily be translated to accommodate the large number of Spanish-speaking employees.

As a result, Veach's staff has developed its own retirement-planning workshop for use beginning in mid-1980. It concentrates on the same general topics as the AIM package but reduces the number of sessions to seven. These two-hour meetings include film strips, debates, and role-playing and retirement games to get people talking. Typical topics for a debate might be whether or not to move after retirement, or if one should try a second career. The staff has developed a Monopoly type of board game in the shape of an enormous L, complete with jean buttons for markers, bright green dice and a stack of question-and-answer cards which are backed with the famous Levi Strauss logo. The board directions return players to "start" for forgetting to sign up for Social Security, but reward them with a four-space advance when they enroll in a first aid class at the local hospital. The game is called Discovery Unlimited. Some typical questions from the Q and A cards are:

"Can you arrange to have your Social Security check deposited directly to your bank account?" (Answer—Yes.)

"What is the earliest you can retire from Levi Strauss? (Age 55 with 15 years of continuous service.)

"Name three of the community property states." (California, Texas, Nevada, Louisiana, Idaho, Arizona, New Mexico, Washington.)

"What amount of emergency money should you set aside before retirement?" (Three months' income.)

"Can you request a pension estimate before you decide to retire?" (Yes. Call Retirement Services/ Employee Benefits Department.)

"Can you name some areas in which you might expect to have a reduction in expenses after retirement?" (Commutation costs, lunches, clothing.)

As part of its general approach to the job-related anxieties of aging, the retirement services group is working on a manual for managers which will serve as a kind of sensitivity training for supervisors. The aim here, Veach says, is to try to convince managers to spend extra time with older workers who are having difficulties or are not performing up to standard, and to make them more aware of the pressures on the person who is approaching the final segment of the work life. Where an individual employee is displaying a significant problem integrating with younger workers, company policy is to help that person with an appropriate workshop or one-to-one counseling, which is available.

POLAROID CORPORATION

Polaroid combines individual counseling and formal seminars in its comprehensive approach to preretirement planning. Four years ago, Joseph S. Perkins, corporate retirement administrator, started seeing employees 54 years of age and older at their request and has personally held more than 300 counseling sessions annually with individual workers and their spouses. Each of these sessions averages two hours. Perkins updates the information between three and five years after the initial session. During the 18 months prior to retirement he spends between four and eight hours with the employee discussing attitudes toward retirement, use of time, the difficulties of transition, suitable retirement activities, and financial information. This latter area includes data about benefits and how to budget and survive in an inflationary economy. Perkins says he stresses reality, does not try to paint a rosy picture, admits that the transition to retirement is not easy, and bases his approach on the "dignity of choice." He feels that somewhere between 10 and 25 percent of the people he counsels continue working because of this realistic approach.

In addition, Polaroid offers a six-part evening seminar twice a year, which is held at the company's conference center. Each session is organized topically and covers one of the following subjects: finances, legal matters, Social Security, Polaroid's retirement plans, good life habits, and future interests and activities. This last session is run by Henry Pearson, a retiree himself, and concentrates on skills identification, second careers, and the best use of leisure time. A cafeteria approach is used; employees can come to one, two or all six meetings, or can pick up a few in the spring and others the following fall. Perkins deliberately arranged for evening seminars to make it easier for working spouses to attend. About 700 of Polaroid's 14,000 employees are over 59 and eligible for the seminar. The company draws approximately 120 people per session, excluding spouses, and has had to turn some of the overflow crowd away because of lack of room. Perkins feels these sessions must be having an impact.

The company's average retirement age is 62. In the past, of those who worked until age 65, close to 50 percent would stay on. Last year Perkins noticed that 70 percent of the 65-year-olds decided to continue working. He points out that this one year's experience should not be overemphasized. It certainly cannot be called a trend. Nor is it possible to determine the relative importance of inflation, personal considerations, the preretirement counseling, or the fact that Polaroid employees retain the full range of benefits, including accrual of the pension, after age 65.

ATLANTIC RICHFIELD COMPANY

Atlantic Richfield, a domestic integrated energy company, has a work force of 50,000 at large and small locations around the nation. Prior to the passage of the Age Discrimination in Employment Act (ADEA) amendment, ARCO had advanced mandatory retirement for its employees to the age of 70. As part of its commitment to career/life planning, the company instituted three pilot preretirement programs in 1977. ARCO used the Action for Independent Maturity (AIM) program in Dallas, which was led by a staff member who had attended an AIM seminar training program. The individual sessions were amplified by experts in Social Security, finance, taxes, and the law from the local area. The Retirement Advisers

Program was used in Los Angeles. This is a series of lectures given by one expert, who also draws on community resource people. In Philadelphia, ARCO Chemical developed an independent workshop similar to the AIM program, in conjunction with the local chamber of commerce.

Management analyzed the advantages, disadvantages, and costs of all three approaches, as well as employee reactions to the different formats. They found that while the lecture approach produces the most information it makes it more difficult to keep people's attention than the workshop format. Nevertheless, employees in all three programs wanted as much detailed financial information as possible, and were keenly interested in the tax implications of their retirement benefits. All the programs had strengths and weaknesses and none was completely suitable either for ARCO's varied work force or the company's diverse locations. This led Atlantic Richfield to consider developing its own videotapes, which would become the core of its life/preretirement planning program. The advantage of the tapes, according to the manager of employee relations, policies, and procedures, is that they can be used alone at the smaller company facilities, or supplemented with case materials, workshops, lectures, and experts where such expansion is indicated.

ARCO is investigating other aspects of life/preretirement planning. It is a client of the Second Career Program in Los Angeles and is considering doing a survey of its recently retired population to determine if there is a difference in adjustment to retirement between those who have gone through the pilot programs and those who have not.

MORGAN GUARANTY TRUST COMPANY OF NEW YORK

Morgan Guaranty started a formal program of preretirement planning in mid-1977. This two-day seminar was first offered to those closest to the bank's normal retirement age of 65 and is conducted by members of the personnel department. It includes detailed financial data about retirement benefits, a speaker from the Social Security Administration who explains Social Security benefits and Medicare, and a film called *A Week Full of Saturdays*, which presents three approaches to retirement—someone who decides to continue working, an individual who moves to a retirement community, and a younger couple who are just beginning the planning process. It is intended to provoke discussion about choices.

The seminar is limited to 20 people, and is run during regular working hours. By 1979 employees age 63 and up were eligible, giving those whose retirement is scheduled for 1981 two years in which to prepare. The eventual aim is to start retirement planning at 55.

The seminar also makes available financial, estate planning, and budgeting information on a group basis. Initially the seminar included speakers from employment agencies which handle part-time placement, but this was abandoned after seminar participants showed little interest.

The preretirement program has been extremely well received by the participants, who fill out an evaluation questionnaire. Suggestions for improvement have centered on a desire for more information about benefits, profit sharing, and Social Security, and these areas have been amplified accordingly. The seminar emphasizes choice, but according to assistant vice-president Arthur Barkman, it is too soon to determine whether the program is having an effect on individual retirement decisions. There are many other considerations at work. Most of the bank's benefit plans are tied to length of service. For example, after ten years an employee is eligible for life insurance equal to one year's salary and some people extend their employment to qualify. Others continue working to accrue additional pension credits, or to join their 1000 colleagues who have made it into Morgan's "Quarter Century" club. In 1979, 11 of those reaching age 65 decided to stay on, which was 20 percent of the employees eligible for normal retirement.

GRUMMAN AEROSPACE CORPORATION

As we mentioned earlier, Daniel Knowles, personnel director at Grumman, has pointed out that the immediate effect of the age extension amendment is to shift the matter of choice about retirement from the company to the worker. Knowles believes that employees cannot make this decision intelligently without extensive information and counseling. For the last 15 years, the Benefacts Company has provided Grumman employees with a yearly individualized statement on their health and life insurance, pension and Social Security benefits, and investment planning. In addition, a special report goes to all workers 55 and over. This supplies pension-benefit figures if the employee retires at 55, 58, 62, or 65 and describes the various pension options an employee can choose. One is the survivors' benefit pop-up clause, which permits an employee who has taken the survivors' benefit to revert to full pension if his or her spouse dies before retirement takes place. Another is the level income option, which allows early retirees a larger pension payment until they qualify for Social Security. Also included is a Social Security forecast and an employee investment table for ages 55, 62, and 65.

In 1978 the Benefacts organization decided to get into the preretirement planning act using Grumman as a guinea pig. Knowles was curious to see if preretirement group counseling could be provided in a nonthreatening manner, and he wanted to test the differences in response of people at ages 55, 60, and 64. Accordingly, three voluntary experimental courses were set up, differentiated only by the targeted age groups. Employees were invited to attend an evening session with their spouses. They received the detailed special report and participated in a two-hour session on retirement problems and adjustments. They were given a tape recorder, six hours of tapes, and accompanying workbooks prepared by Benefacts, and were asked to listen to the material over the next six weeks and answer the workbook questions. The subjects included Social Security, pensions, investments, recreation, insurance, and health. A second group meeting was scheduled after the six-week period and included experts from the Social Security Administration, as well as Grumman's administrators of pensions, benefits, and investments and a Grumman annuitant. The group watched a film about Social Security, received a handout of the most frequently asked retirement queries, had a question-and-answer exchange with the authorities, and gave a written evaluation of the material and format. Knowles stressed throughout that this was a service designed to give employees pertinent information so that they could make educated choices, not a way to get people to retire. The participants' reaction was favorable to the design, content, and purpose of the course.

Knowles noticed only minor differences among the groups.

Index